D0836057

# HOW TO BE POLITE IN JAPANESE

Osamu Mizutani and Nobuko Mizutani

日本語の敬語

THE JAPAN TIMES, LTD.
TOKYO, JAPAN
1987

First edition, February 1987
All rights reserved.
Copyright © 1987 by Osamu Mizutani and Nobuko Mizutani
Cover art by Atelier Hirata.
Editorial assistance and indexing
by Janet Ashby.
For information, write: The Japan Times, Ltd.
5-4, Shibaura 4-chome, Minato-ku, Tokyo 108, Japan.

ISBN 4-7890-0338-9

Published in Japan by The Japan Times, Ltd.

PRINTED IN JAPAN

# PREFACE

Japanese ideas of politeness have developed within a closed society, relatively speaking. People have lived in close quarters generation after generation, sharing the same values and being careful not to hurt others. The constant use of *aizuchi,* the finishing up of what another person has started to say, the frequent expression of concern about others — these have developed in a homogeneous society.

However, now and in the future the Japanese also face the necessity of communicating with foreigners and, even more importantly, with other Japanese whom they do not know well. They can no longer expect others to share the same values or the same set of experiences. They have to be more specific and clear in their self-expression, and be more ready to state their own opinions.

But this does not mean that polite Japanese will fall out of use or prove to be totally unsuited to a new age. On the contrary, it will be even more effective in communications between persons who do not know each other well. Consideration towards others will be the paramount factor in communications in the future, and polite language in Japanese is in essence the expression of consideration towards others.

January 1987
Osamu and Nobuko Mizutani

iii

# ACKNOWLEDGMENTS

We take pleasure in publishing a book on how to be polite in Japanese. Since the publication of "An Introduction to Modern Japanese" and "Nihongo Notes," we have met many foreigners wishing to know how to speak and behave politely in Japanese. Urged on by their enthusiasm, we have worked on this matter, and tried to explain it as systematically as possible.

We wish to express our gratitude to the many people who have made this book possible. Such institutions as the Japan Foundation, the YMCA English School, the English Language Education Council and the Japan Association of Language Teachers provided Nobuko Mizutani with a chance to speak about this matter in English, and the audiences attending the lectures raised many stimulating questions. And we would also like to indicate our gratitude to Janet Ashby, who carefully corrected the English and gave us valuable suggestions.

# CONTENTS

* * *

An asterisk has been used to indicate ungrammatical or inappropriate sentences: "Polite forms in modifying phrases, as in *Kore-wa kinoo kaimashita hon desu (This is a book I bought yesterday), are understood but sound strange and foreign."

## Note Concerning Romanization

The romanization used in this book is based on the Hepburn system with the following modifications.

1. When the same vowel occurs consecutively, the letter is repeated rather than using the "⁻" mark.
   ex. *Tookyoo* (instead of *Tōkyō*)
2. The sound indicated by the hiragana ん is written with "*n*" regardless of what sound follows it.
   ex. *shinbun* (instead of shimbun)
   ex. *shinpai* (instead of shimpai)

The words connected with hyphens are pronounced as one unit.
   ex. *genki-desu*
   ex. *Soo-desu-ne*

# INTRODUCTION: POLITENESS IN JAPANESE

## 1. Present-day Polite Language in Japan

*Keigo,* the polite language in Japanese, has various aspects, but one has to limit one's discussion in a small book like this. The subject of discussion is therefore limited here to that of present-day *keigo* in Japan and to its use in spoken language (including short notes and greeting cards).

**changes in *keigo*** There is a great difference between *keigo* before and after World War II, as postwar Japanese society has become highly democratized in language as well as other areas. The following is a list of the major changes in postwar *keigo.*

1) Special polite terms used for referring to the emperor and his family members have been abolished. Now in public reporting such as newspapers and television or radio news, a minimum polite wording is used for the imperial family. Before and during the war special terms were used to refer to the emperor and his family — for instance, when the emperor went out the special term *gyookoo* (His Majesty's visit) was used. But now *oide-ni naru* (one goes — polite) is used instead of *gyookoo,* and in referring to other actions as well, usually the *-areru* form (as in *yomareru*) or the *o . . . ni naru* form (as in *oyomi-ni naru*) is used. These polite wordings are not different from those commonly used in daily conversation when referring to one's acquaintances politely.

2) Terms referring to oneself and terms of respect referring to others have been tremendously simplified. Before the war a dozen different terms — *watakushi, atakushi, atashi, atai, ore, washi, wagahai, temae, shoosee, kochitora,* etc. — were used to refer to oneself, but now just a few terms, such as *watashi, boku,* and *ore,*

1

are used in most cases. Terms of respect for family members were also numerous and complicated before and during the war, but now have been simplified.

3) Wide discrepancies have disappeared. There used to be great differences in politeness of language between two different social classes such as between bosses and workers, customers and salesmen; but now the former talk more politely, and the latter less politely, than before. In a word, the Japanese people have today reached a high degree of equality in language usage.

4) Gender differences in language usage have been minimized. Some very feminine expressions have disappeared since the war. Young women now seldom use such expressions as *Shiranakute-yo* (I don't know) and *Dekinai koto-yo* (I can't do that) in familiar speech; such expressions as *odekake-asobashimashita* (he went out) for *odekake-ni narimashita* are also seldom heard in polite female speech. At the same time, men's speech has become more refined and, in a way, closer to feminine speech. Men add the honorific "*o*" to more words now than before: *ocha* and *okashi* are more common than *cha* and *kashi*, and *obentoo*, *okane* and *osake* are now used by many men.

5) However age differences have not undergone as much change. Older people are still referred to and spoken to politely even in present-day society. Probably this aspect has undergone the least amount of change.

And generational differences are very strong even now. Young students speak politely to students a year or two ahead of them. This is discussed in more detail in the next section, "Factors deciding the level of politeness" (*cf. senpai, koohai*).

All in all postwar polite Japanese has become much less complicated than before, but this probably does not mean that much to those who are studying Japanese as a foreign language. To them, the Japanese system of expressing politeness must seem very complicated. In this book we will try to analyze being polite in

Japanese and present it in a clear and simple way; in the process we must unfortunately ignore points that are not commonly needed in daily life or that are limited to a certain group or locality. However, we believe that foreigners can understand any subtle point whatever in Japanese and can use it if they so desire; we do not believe in a "gaijin Japanese" different from the Japanese of native speakers.

## 2. Factors Deciding the Level of Politeness

### (1) Familiarity

The first factor in deciding the level of speech is, as in the case of English, degree of acquaintance or intimacy. Namely, when one speaks to a stranger or when one meets someone for the first time, one uses the polite form.

**introducing oneself** When you are introduced to someone, you will use the polite form as in

> Hajimemashite. Jonson-desu. Doozo yoroshiku. (Glad to meet you. I'm Mr./Mrs./Miss Johnson.)

**telephone** When you answer a telephone call, you usually say

> Moshimoshi, Jonson-desu.

or even

> Moshimoshi, Jonson-de gozaimasu.

because you don't know to whom you are talking.

When a Japanese answers a phone, he often says something like

> Moshimoshi, Takahashi-desu.

Then, if he finds out that he is talking with an old friend of his, he will suddenly change his tone as in

3

*E, donata-desu-ka. . . . Yamada-san? Takeshi? Naanda, kimi-ka.* (May I ask who I'm talking to? Mr. Yamada? Takeshi (first name)? Oh, it's you!)

**public speaking** Needless to say, one uses the polite form when speaking to the general public. A television or radio announcer always uses the polite form, as in

*Konbanwa, shichiji-no nyuusu-desu.* (Good evening. It's seven o'clock, time for today's news.)

*Kyoo-wa kono mondai-o toriageru koto-ni shimashita.* (This topic will be discussed today.)

## (2) Age

The second factor is age. As a rule, older people talk in a familiar way toward younger people and younger people talk politely to older people. Among people of the same age familiar conversation is common.

**children** Children below a certain age, namely when they are not yet socially trained, use the plain form to everyone regardless of age. Some parents start training them to talk politely to others before they go to elementary school, but an average child doesn't start trying to talk politely until after entering elementary school at the age of six.

**elementary school** School classmates start using familiar speech among themselves from the very beginning because they are regarded as knowing each other well by virtue of belonging to the same class. Generally speaking, children are socially trained in terms of speech during the six years of elementary school, and when they finish this they start using polite forms toward older persons and those they do not know well.

**family terms** They also start using different family terms depending on to whom they are talking. Namely they say *chichi*

4

(my father) instead of *otoosan* (Daddy) and *haha* (my mother) instead of *okaasan* (Mommie) when referring to their parents in social situations.

**senpai, koohai**    Although classmates are regarded as being on exactly the same level, students who are one year ahead in school are considered to be older and superior. The word *senpai* refers to those who are ahead of one either in school or at work. If persons are even one year senior to you, you have to use the polite form to them.

**students**    The *senpai-koohai* relationship is surprisingly strong among Japanese students. Especially among students belonging to the same group in sports or some other activity, *senpai* are regarded as absolutely superior and *koohai* have to obey them unconditionally. On the other hand, *senpai* are supposed to teach *koohai* kindly and be as protective toward them as an older brother or even a parent. This is not limited to male students; woman have similar relations, especially among those who belong to the same sports team.

The levels of speech are quite different among *senpai* and *koohai*; a *senpai* uses the plain form and a *koohai* uses the polite form. This distinction is usually strictly observed, sometimes more so than between teachers and students.

**workers**    The *senpai-koohai* relation is also seen in companies and other workplaces. Those who enter later are regarded as *koohai* who should respect their *senpai.* Needless to say, the degree of strictness with which this distinction is observed varies depending on the group; generally speaking, the distinction is more strict in organizations of larger scale.

When *koohai* are actually senior in age, it is difficult for a *senpai* to decide how to talk to them. In this case both the factors of age and of social relations have to be considered, and in fact frequently more than one factor is involved when one decides on the degree of politeness of one's speech.

## (3) Social relations

The third factor is social relations. Social relations here refers to such relationships as those between employers and employees, customers and salesmen, and teachers and students. This might also be called "professional relations."

Generally speaking, those who are of higher status, such as employers, customers, and teachers, will use either the plain form or the polite form, while those of lower status use the polite form.

**boss & worker**     In some cases, both bosses and their men use plain forms, but usually bosses are spoken to politely. In big enterprises bosses often use polite forms. An average businessman — *sarariiman* in Japanese — will use polite forms towards his boss and plain forms towards fellow workers of a similar age.

Here also, the age factor has to be considered. Namely, a boss will often use polite forms toward a worker who is older, depending on the situation. If the boss is required to act in terms of social relations, he will use the plain form. For instance, when the department chief is present, a section chief will use the plain form toward his men regardless of their age, but when the section chief is alone with an older worker, or when they are outside the company having tea together, he is likely to use the polite form.

**customer & salesman**     Between customers and salesmen, the basic principle is superior and inferior; salesmen are supposed to use polite language towards customers. But there are several other factors which are also used when deciding degree of politeness.

**(price)**     Generally speaking, those who sell costly merchandise talk more politely than those who sell inexpensive articles. Salesmen who deal with merchandise such as jewels, cars, and expensive clothes talk very politely. On the other hand, fish and vegetable sellers use a rather rough language.

The same salesman can change language depending on the price of the merchandise. Just recently, a teacher of Japanese we know carried out a small investigation. She accompanied tens of foreign students visiting real estate offices to find rooms to rent. The students wanted to find apartments renting for about 30,000 yen a month, and the real estate agents always spoke to them using the plain form. However, an acquaintance of ours who was looking for a place for about 300,000 yen reports that the real estate agents spoke very politely to her.

**(familiarity)** In the case of daily transactions in cheaper articles, the factor of familiarity also enters into deciding the level of speech. This is probably because people used to, and generally still do, buy daily merchandise in the neighborhood.

**(age)** When the customer is a child, the age factor is at work, and the salesclerk will use the plain form.

**(kinds of merchandise)** Sometimes the level of speech has somehow been traditionally set by occupation.

First, bank clerks are always polite while clerks at post offices often use the plain form. One reason may be that post offices deal with customers from the neighborhood and another may be that they are mostly run by the government, although government workers are recently trying to be friendly and polite towards the public.

**(taxi)** Some taxi drivers talk politely to their customers but most of them are quite blunt. Although some taxi companies are trying to instruct their drivers to talk politely, most customers still have the idea that taxi drivers are supposed to talk somewhat roughly. Somehow there is a general understanding that they are allowed to use the plain form.

**(restaurant)** Polite language is used in expensive restaurants and familiar speech in inexpensive ones. Some sushi shops are quite expensive, but the speech may not sound very polite. There is a general understanding that speech should be brisk among those who deal with food that easily spoils.

**(salesmen's greetings)** A shop worker usually greets customers when they come in with

7

*Irasshaimase.* (Welcome.)

or sometimes, more briefly,

*Irasshai!*

but the customer usually remains silent. This may strike foreigners as strange. (Some Japanese also feel ill at ease with this; they will say something like *Konnichiwa* (Good day), *Konbanwa* (Good evening) or *Doomo* (Hello).)

This should be considered to be a social practice somewhat like a stage drama, with the worker acting the role of a servant and the customer that of a lord. This has nothing to do with social standing; to prove this, a sushi cook who today greets customers politely and is ignored will go into another sushi shop tomorrow when taking his day off, be greeted politely, and ignore this greeting.

Those who feel ill at ease with this custom may answer with *Konnichiwa*, *Konbanwa* or *Doomo.* And when leaving a restaurant after a meal, a customer can either say nothing at all or say

*Gochisoosama.* (Thank you for the good meal.)

or

*Doomo.*

which can mean "Thank you very much."


## (4) Social status

People of a certain social standing are usually spoken to and referred to politely. In prewar Japan members of the aristocracy such as dukes, earls, and the emperor and his family members were spoken to and referred to with special polite terms.

**the emperor** Especially in referring to the emperor, various special terms were in use before World War II, but now the emperor and his family members are reported about in the mass media with the minimum level of polite terms. Before and during the war the emperor's visit somewhere was referred to in such special terms as *gyookoo*, which was used only for the emperor (for the empress and the crown prince, a different special term, *gyookee*, was used). Now a visit by the emperor is reported with *oide-ni narimashita* or *ikaremashita*, adding the polite suffix *-rareru*. Except in the case of the emperor and his family members, no special expressions of respect are now used in public reporting.

**high social standing**　　As far as public reporting, both written and oral, is concerned, all people are thus treated equally with the exception of the emperor and his family. But in daily conversation, certain occupations are still treated with respect. Such persons as medical doctors, high-ranking government officials, statesmen, university professors, and company directors are usually spoken to politely.

**indirect influence**　　But the idea of social status affects the use of language in an indirect way. People often try to adopt what is regarded as the linguistic custom of the upper classes. Since families in the upper classes are thought to use polite terms toward elder members, some parents try to train their children to use such polite speech, especially in the presence of others. Thus, even in a household where everybody uses plain forms, when a visitor comes the mother makes the children use the polite forms towards their parents and she will talk politely to her husband.

## (5) Gender

Besides familiarity, age, social relations and social standing, there are several other factors that come into play in language usage, and gender is one of them.

Speech tends to be more familiar between people of the same sex than between men and women. This is especially true with older people who were brought up and educated with members of their own sex. (Differences between men's and women's speech are discussed in more detail in Part II.)

9

## (6) Group membership

**in-group and out-group distinctions**    The Japanese use different expressions and terms of respect when referring to others depending on to whom they are talking. This is not limited to the case of Japanese. In English too, one refers to one's own wife or husband in different ways depending on the situation; you might use your wife's name when speaking about her with a friend, but use the term "Mother" or "Mommie" when speaking with your children. However, this distinction is a little more complicated in Japanese.

**in-group family terms**    Older family members should be addressed with terms of respect, as in

| | | |
|---|---|---|
| *Otoosan* (Father) | *Otoosama* (Father, more polite) | *Otoochan* (Daddy, more familiar) |
| *Okaasan* (Mother) | *Okaasama* (Mother, more polite) | *Okaachan* (Mommie, more familiar) |
| *Oniisan* (Older brother) | *Oniisama* (more polite) | *Oniichan* (more familiar) |
| *Oneesan* (Older sister) | *Oneesama* (more polite) | *Oneechan* (more familiar) |

In addressing younger family members, their first name or their first name plus "*san*" or "*chan*" is used, as in

| | | |
|---|---|---|
| Yoshio (boy's name) | Yoshio-*san* (more polite) | Yoshio-*chan* (more familiar) |
| Kazuko (girl's name) | Kazuko-*san* (more polite) | Kazuko-*chan* (more familiar) |

**out-group family terms**    The above terms are not always used when referring to family members in conversation with non-family members; only in the following situations are they used in the same way:

(1)   when the listener is a very close friend

(2)   when the speaker is a child and has not reached the age when such distinctions are expected.

Otherwise one has to use the terms found below.

*chichi*   (my father)

*haha*   (my mother)
*ani*    (my older brother)
*ane*   (my older sister)
*otooto* (my younger brother) — or his name
*imooto* (my younger sister) — or her name

No terms of respect such as "*san*" are added.

**identification with the family**   This distinction is based on the idea that one should identify oneself with one's family. Therefore when talking with others about one's family, one refers to them just as one would refer to oneself. This means that one does not use polite expressions when referring to them, just as it would sound strange if you used polite language about yourself.

Thus when speaking with an acquaintance, one does not say something like

*\*Otoosan-wa ima uchi-ni irasshaimasen.* (Father is not at home now — *irasshaimasen* is an expression of respect.)

This sentence is perfectly all right if used to refer to someone else's father. Or it can also be used if you are talking to your child, as in

CHILD:  *Otoosan-wa?* (Where's Father?)
MOTHER: *Ima uchi-ni irasshaimasen-yo.* (He's not at home now.)

NEIGHBOR: *Otoosan, irasshaimasen-ka.* (Isn't your father at home?)
YOU:  *Ima orimasen. Haha-nara orimasu-ga.* (No, he's not at home. My mother's home, though — *orimasen, orimasu* are humble expressions.)

This is not limited to the form of expression but also applies to the content of what one should say about one's family. For instance, one does not usually praise members of one's own family in conversation with acquaintances, nor does one freely accept compliments on them from others. This can easily be understood if one

11

remembers that one is supposed to identify oneself with one's family.

**identification with an organization** This distinction made when speaking with those inside and outside one's group is not limited to family members, but is extended to organizations to which one belongs — usually the company for which one works.

Suppose you telephone the director of a company, for instance, saying

> *Moshimoshi, shachoo-san, irasshaimasu-ka.* (Hello, is the director there?)

His secretary will answer either

> *Hai, orimasu.* (Yes, he is.)

or

> *Iie, ima orimasen-ga.* (I'm sorry, but he's out.)

She will use humble expressions like *"orimasu"* and *"orimasen."* The director is her boss within the company and she will use polite expressions when talking with him directly, but she uses humble expressions when talking with someone from outside the company.

In such cases terms of respect are not used. Company employees refer to their director as *"Shachoo"* (Director) or Yamada without adding *"san,"* as in

> *Shachoo-wa mamonaku modorimasu.* (The director will be back shortly.)

> *Yamada-wa ima dekakete-orimasu.* (Yamada is out now.)

And if someone should ask to speak with Mr. Yamada, the section chief, as in

> *Moshimoshi, Yamada-san-ni onegai-shimasu.*

one of the members of his section will say something like

12

*Yamada-desu-ka. Chotto omachi-kudasai.* (I will get Yamada for you. Please wait a moment.)

This is because one identifies oneself with the company where one works. One's colleagues are regarded as a kind of family; therefore even a young secretary will refer to the director of her company without any terms of respect when talking with someone from outside. This is like referring to one's father as "*chichi*" (my father) rather than "*Otoosan*" (Father) in social situations.

**degree of identification** This identification with a company is common but not as common as identifying oneself with family members. The degree of identification with the organization one works for varies depending on the organization. Generally speaking, workers in larger and more conservative organizations have a stronger sense of identification with them. In organizations where people's sense of union is loose, such as schools and hospitals, clerks will use polite terms to refer to teachers and doctors even when speaking with out-group persons. If you say on the telephone

*Yamada-sensee, onegai-shimasu.* (May I speak to Professor/Dr. Yamada, please?)

a clerk or nurse will say

*Ima irasshaimasen.* (He's not here now — *irasshaimasen* is an expression of respect.)

rather than saying

*Ima orimasen.*

Since the degree of identification differs from one organization to another, some training in this matter is usually required. In large companies it is common to set aside a few weeks of the training period for new employees to teach them an appropriate way of speaking.

13

## (7) Situation

People also change levels of speech depending on the situation, even when talking with the same person. When two people have a falling-out with each other, they often change their language. There are two types of change — from polite to familiar and from familiar to polite. The former is less sophisticated than the latter. In quarrels, unsophisticated speakers start calling each other bad names and using rough language, while sophisticated speakers use polite language. Changing to a more polite language shows that the speaker no longer has close relations with the listener.

Women, who are usually more linguistically conscious than men, tend to follow the latter course. Very often an angry wife will start talking very politely. When she wants to return to her parents' home after a quarrel with her husband, instead of saying

> *Kaeru-wa.* (I'm going home — familiar)

or

> *Kaerimasu.* (I'm going home — polite)

she will use very polite expressions like

> *Kaerasete-itadakimasu.* (With your permission, I'd like to be excused and go home — very polite.)

# 3. Verbal and Nonverbal Politeness

**apologizing for rudeness**　　Politeness must be expressed by all of one's actions; using polite verbal expressions correctly is just part of being polite in Japanese. To be fully polite one is expected to always reflect on one's actions and ask oneself if one has not been rude unintentionally. Thus the Japanese frequently use apologetic expressions such as *Sumimasen* (I'm sorry), *Shitsuree-shimashita* (Excuse me — I have been rude) and *Gomen-kudasai* (Excuse me).

14

**following the appropriate steps** In addition to verbally asking for forgiveness for one's rudeness, one should also try to minimize the trouble one might cause by talking to someone. Thus, one must go through the appropriate steps when starting a conversation and developing it. One should first attract the other person's attention and then in due course indicate the purpose of one's conversation. This process will be explained further in Part I, but if one is merely fluent in verbal expressions and neglects going through the proper steps one will sound very rude, even ruder than a clumsy speaker. The Japanese in fact tend to value the nonverbal expression of politeness more highly than verbal politeness. Thus a speaker who is not very fluent but shows a polite hesitancy and fear of being rude will often be warmly received.

**tone** The tone of speech is also very important in sounding polite. In Japanese conversation, a hesitant tone indicates reserve while sounding too definite when giving one's opinion can seem aggressive. This will also be treated more fully in Part I.

**body language** Nonverbal behavior such as bowing, handing things over to others, and keeping an appropriate distance from the listener is also important in conveying a polite attitude. If these are not used properly, one can be impolite without meaning to do so. This will be discussed in the last section of Part I.

15

# PART I POLITENESS IN ATTITUDE

## 1. How to Talk Politely

(1) *Aizuchi*

**frequent response** When two Japanese converse, the listener frequently gives short reply words like *Ee*, *Hai*, *Soo-desu-ne*, and *Naruhodo*. For example, when the speaker says

> *Kinoo Hakone-e ikimashitara* . . . (When I went to Hakone yesterday)

the listener says

> *Ee.*

Then the speaker continues

> . . . *midori-ga kiree-deshita-ga* . . . (the green leaves were beautiful but)

and the listener says

> *Ee, ee.*

Then the speaker says

> . . . *kuruma-ga ookute* . . . (there were so many cars)

and the listener says

> *Aa, soo-deshoo-ne.* (That must be so.)

Then the speaker concludes his sentence by saying

> . . . *taihen-deshita-yo.* (We had a hard time.)

17

The listener now says

> *Soo-desu-ka. Jitsu-wa watashi-mo kyonen Hakone-e ikimashita-ga* . . . (Is that right? As a matter of fact I too went to Hakone last year.)

Then the former speaker listens saying

> *Ee, ee.*

**aizuchi** These reply words are called *aizuchi*. *Aizuchi* are not quite replies; they are given as a sign to show that the listener is listening attentively and has understood so far, and to encourage the speaker to go on. Therefore saying *Ee* or *Hai* does not necessarily mean "yes" or "I agree with you." Sometimes foreigners take these reply words for expressions of agreement and are unpleasantly surprised to find out that they are not.

**what does aizuchi mean?** The word *aizuchi* comes from two swordsmiths hammering a blade in turn. The word *ai* means "doing something together," as in such words as *aite* (a person to do something with, like *hanashi-aite* — a person to talk with; *kekkon-aite* — a person to marry; and *soodan-aite* — a person to consult with), or *aiseki* (sitting at the same table in a restaurant) and several others; *tsuchi* means "a hammer" (*tsuchi* becomes *zuchi* when combined with *ai*). Two people talking and frequently exchanging response words is thus likened to the way two swordsmiths hammer on a blade.

18

**the function of *aizuchi*** In Japanese conversation, the listener constantly helps the speaker with *aizuchi*, and the speaker is always conscious of the listener's *aizuchi* — the roles of the speaker and the listener are not completely separated. This use of constant *aizuchi* in the flow of conversation can be likened to the use of commas and periods in the written language. Thus *aizuchi* are essential in Japanese conversation, and they have to be given correctly in order to communicate properly in Japanese.

**how to give *aizuchi*** *Aizuchi* must be given in a way such that they do not interfere with the flow of speech. They are usually spoken softly and have to be given at the right moment, namely exactly when the speaker expects them. A speaker asks for *aizuchi* by slowing down in the last part of the phrase and saying it with a dangling intonation. For instance, instead of saying

> *Kinoo odenwa-shimashita-ga.* (I called yesterday)

he says

> *Kinoo odenwa-shi-ma-shi-ta-ga* . . . .

If you give *aizuchi* before the speaker does this, he will feel that you want him to stop talking. In other words, this is equivalent to saying, "All right, all right. That's enough."

**words used as *aizuchi*** The most common words used as *aizuchi* are *hai, ee, un, haa, naruhodo, soo-desu-ka,* and *soo-deshoo-ne*. *Hai* is used in polite conversation, *ee* is most often used in informal conversation, and *un* is used only in familiar talk. *Haa* is a variant of *hai*.

Sometimes these words are repeated to show enthusiasm as in "*Hai, hai*"; "*Ee, ee*"; or "*un, un.*" *Naruhodo* is used mainly by men, but avoided in polite speech. *Soo-desu-ka* (Is that right?) and *Soo-deshoo-ne* (That must be so) are also used often.

Besides these words, various exclamations such as *hoo, hee, aa,* and *huun* are used.

Sometimes the listener changes his *aizuchi* words from more polite ones to less polite ones to show that he is so absorbed in what the speaker is saying that he has forgotten all considerations of politeness.

**frequency of *aizuchi***   The average number of *aizuchi* per minute is, disregarding individual differences, about 20 — from 12 to 26, according to a study made by one of the authors. Since the average number of syllables per minute of speech is about 400, an average listener gives *aizuchi* every 20 syllables or so.

There are individual and situational differences. Some people give more *aizuchi* than others; those leading a discussion or conducting an interview, for example, will give *aizuchi* more frequently.

The fact that an average listener gives *aizuchi* every 20 syllables is significant, as many sentences have a length of about 20 syllables and in longer sentences people generally pause after a phrase of about 20 syllables. For instance,

> *Senjitsu-wa taihen gochisoosama-deshita.* (Thank you very much for the nice meal the other day.)

has 18 syllables.

> *Shinkansen-ni notte-itara jishin-ga atte . . .* (When I was riding on the Shinkansen, there was an earthquake and . . .)

has 20 syllables.

After listening to phrases like these, the average listener will give *aizuchi*. And the speaker softens and slows his tone when expecting *aizuchi*. This can be shown as follows.

Sometimes *aizuchi* are given before the last part of the phrase is completed.

**absence of *aizuchi*** When two people are conversing and giving *aizuchi* regularly, the absence of *aizuchi* will mean that the listener has not understood or does not want to continue the conversation. Therefore, Japanese speakers will start worrying if someone listens quietly without giving *aizuchi* when expected. They will especially feel uneasy at the absence of *aizuchi* when speaking on the telephone, because they are unable to see the listener's facial expression. They will soon start sounding uneasy and repeat "*moshimoshi.*"

In polite conversation, one often indicates a lack of understanding with facial expression as well as the absence of *aizuchi* rather than by verbally telling the speaker that one has not understood. In this way the absence of *aizuchi* in personal conversation means the existence of some difficulty in communication.

**aizuchi and foreigners** Although *aizuchi* are essential for conversing in Japanese effectively, foreigners often find it difficult to become used to them. It requires training and effort to become able to give *aizuchi* properly.

The first step is to understand that *aizuchi* are NOT interruption but rather encouragement; the next step is to try to give *aizuchi* oneself. For those who find it extremely difficult to give verbal *aizuchi*, nodding can serve as *aizuchi* as long as one is not speaking on the phone. In fact, some Japanese use nodding instead of verbal *aizuchi*. Especially when more than one person is listening, the main listener often gives verbal *aizuchi* while the other persons simply nod.

## (2) Finishing up

**finishing up the speaker's sentences** A Japanese listener sometimes finishes up what the speaker is going to say. For example, to make use of the previous conversation about going to Hakone, after the first person has told about his trip, the second person will say

21

*Jitsu-wa watashi-mo kyonen Hakone-e* . . . (*lit.* In fact, I too last year to Hakone . . .)

then the listener may say

*itta-n-desu-ka.* (you went?)

Thus one sentence, *Jitsu-wa watashi-mo kyonen Hakone-e itta-n-desu*, is completed by two people; the listener completed the unfinished sentence started by the speaker. (In polite conversation, the listener may use different expressions like *irasshatta-n-desu-ka* (you went?) and in familiar conversation more familiar expressions are used.)

**in daily conversation**    Finishing up someone's statement is very common in daily conversation. When the Japanese comment on the weather, they often split one sentence into two:

A: *Kyoo-wa kaze-mo nakute*... (There is no wind today, and . . .)

B: *Ii otenki-desu-ne.* (It's a nice day, isn't it?)

Or, when commenting on spring drawing near, they will talk like this:

A: *Daibu atatakaku natte* ... (It has become much warmer and . . .)

B: *Moo sugu haru-desu-ne.* (Spring is just around the corner.)

**guessing the rest of the sentence**    Finishing up the speaker's sentence is possible only when the rest of the sentence can be guessed. Very often one can guess the rest from the situation. For instance, when someone has talked about going to Hakone and the other person says

*Watashi-mo kyonen Hakone-e* ...

then the first person can guess that "*ikimashita*" should follow the phrase.

22

The use of adverbs that imply a negative statement also enables the listener to guess the rest of the sentence. For instance, if someone has said

*Shigoto-wa amari umaku* . . . (*lit.* The work not very successfully . . .)

the listener will say

*ikimasen-deshita-ka.* (didn't go, right?)

because *amari* usually leads to a negative statement.

**desu and deshita**    Sometimes such words as *desu* and *deshita* are used to finish up the speaker's unfinished sentences. For instance, when a person has said

*Natsu-wa yappari biiru* . . . (*lit.* The best thing to have in summer . . . beer.)

the listener is very likely to say

*desu-ne.* (it is, isn't it?)

In the same way, various other words like *desu* are used. When someone has said

*Senshuu-no kin'yoobi-wa ame* . . . (*lit.* Friday last week . . . rainy.)

the listener is likely to say

*deshita.* (it was)

or

*datta-ne.* (it was, wasn't it? — familiar)

Sometimes such phrases as *da-to omoimasu* (I think it is . . .), *kamo shiremasen* (may be . . .), and *yoona ki-ga shimasu* (it seems to me . . .) are also used in answer. For instance,

A:  *Natsu-wa yappari biiru* . . .

23

B: . . . *da-to omoimasu.*

or

A: *Senshuu-no kin'yoobi-wa ame* . . .

B: . . . *datta yoona ki-ga shimasu.*

**tone used to invite finishing up** When a statement is said in one breath and with no sign of encouraging the listener to say anything, the listener usually does not try to finish the sentence. When the first part of a sentence ends with a sustained tone, the listener either finishes it or gives some *aizuchi.*

**a sign of participation** Finishing up someone's unfinished sentence is usually regarded as impolite in English — an English speaker will do this only when the speaker is obviously looking for help in finding the right word.

In Japanese conversation, however, finishing up someone's statement is often regarded as a sign of interested participation, and consequently considered to be good. This is similar to *aizuchi* in that it is done in order to encourage the speaker.

**different ideas of conversation** This difference comes from different ideas of what a conversation should be. In the English idea of conversation or dialogue, one statement is finished and then another statement follows, but in Japanese conversation, even one statement can be made up by two people.

English: A _____  \_\_\_\_  _____
B  _____  _____

Japanese: A _____ . . _____ . . . _____ . . . \_\_ . . . . . . \_
B

**group conversation** In group conversation one sentence can even be split into more than two parts, as in

A: *Are-wa tashika kyonen* . . . (*lit.* That . . . if my memory is correct last year . . .)

24

B: *Datta yoona ki-ga shimasu . . .* (*lit.* was . . . it seems to me . . .)

C: *Kedo-ne.* (. . . , though.)

(If my memory is correct, that was last year, wasn't it?)

This type of talking is common in conversation among those who share the same feelings about a topic, and it helps build up good relations among them.

**in Kabuki** The extreme expression of this idea can be found in Kabuki plays. You may have heard several actors lined up on the stage say phrases by turns and finally complete a statement. This is called *wari-zerifu* (divided line). To simplify it, it goes like this.

1st actor: *Sorosoro*
2nd actor: *jikan-desu-kara*
3rd actor: *moo*
4th actor: *dekakemashoo.*
(Since it's about time, let's go out.)

This Kabuki practice is a stage technique, but it shows how the Japanese are used to, and like, sharing one statement with other speakers.

## (3) Leaving elements unsaid

**incomplete sentences** You have probably noticed that the Japanese often leave part of their sentences unsaid. For instance, when a complete sentence would go

*Moo jikan-desu-kara dekakemashoo.* (Let's go out since it is time now.)

they often say just

> *Moo jikan-desu-kara* . . . (Since it is time now . . .)

and leave the last part unsaid.

The omitted part is sometimes finished up by the other person, as in

> . . . *dekakemashoo-ka.* (shall we go out?)

and sometimes it is expressed by a nonverbal means like nodding or bowing.

Or, a wife may say to her husband

> *Moo jikan-desu-kedo* . . . (It's time now, but . . .)

implying "don't you have to get ready to go out?"

**inviting the listener to complete a statement**  At first glance, these expressions ending in *kara, node* or *kedo* may seem to be incomplete, and the Japanese may seem to be talking with incomplete sentences or fragmentary expressions.

But these expressions are not incomplete according to the Japanese idea of conversation. The Japanese rather regard it as good to invite the listener to give an opinion or judgment by leaving a certain part of the sentence unsaid.

***kedo* used for asking favors or making suggestions**  When a hostess invites a visitor to come to the table for tea, she will say just

> *Ocha-ga hairimashita-kedo* . . . (*lit.* The tea is ready, but . . .)

implying that she wants the visitor to come to where the tea is served. She leaves out the phrase meaning "please come and have some." (She could also use *kara* instead of *kedo*; while saying *kara* implies that the speaker is asking someone to do a favor as a matter of course, saying *kedo* shows that one is hesitant about making this request.)

26

Or, say someone calls a person at home, and his wife answers the telephone. When asked if her husband is there, she will often say

*Hai, orimasu-kedo* . . . (*lit.* Yes, he is home, but . . .)

By leaving out the last part of the sentence following *kedo,* she is waiting for the other person to continue

*Ja, onegai-shimasu*. (Please let me talk with him.)

**reserved attitude**     Or, when asked if a certain date is convenient, one may say

*Watashi-wa kamaimasen-keredo* . . . (*lit.* It's all right with me, but . . .)

and wait for the other person to propose checking with the others involved. One could complete the sentence by saying

*Watashi-wa kamaimasen-keredo, hoka-no hito-nimo kiite-kudasaimasen-ka.* (It's all right with me, but would you ask the others?)

But it sounds more reserved to not complete the sentence and thereby invite the other person to suggest asking the others on his or her own accord.

Thus, leaving a part of the sentence unsaid so that the listener can supplement it is often more considerate and polite than just going ahead and completing one's own sentence. Many foreigners tend to go on and say everything because they believe that using complete sentences is more polite. But always completing one's own sentences can sound as if one is refusing to let the other person participate in completing a sentence which might better be completed by two people.

**main verbs left out in requests**     Another factor in sounding reserved is to leave out the main verb when making a request. Especially in the case of the adverb *doozo* (please) various verbs are understood and left out. For instance, when a visitor arrives,

27

the host or hostess will say "*Doozo*" meaning "Please come in." After showing the visitor into the room, the host/ess will say "*Doozo*" while offering a *zabuton* or a chair to sit on. When serving tea and cookies, the host/ess will very often simply say "*Doozo*" meaning "Please have some." And when seeing the visitor out, the host/ess will say

*Mata doozo.*

meaning "Please come again."

Thus *doozo* is often used alone without a verb when the speaker's intentions are clear. And to make their intentions clear the Japanese usually bow or use other gestures.

**main verbs left out in set expressions** There are also several set expressions where the main verb is left out, such as

*Doozo yoroshiku (onegai-shimasu).* (How do you do? — *lit.* Please be good to me.)

*Doozo goyukkuri (nasatte-kudasai).* (Please take your time.)

*Doozo oraku-ni (nasatte-kudasai).* (Please relax.)

*Osaki-ni (shitsuree-shimasu).* (Excuse me — said when leaving before someone else.)

**giving a negative evaluation** The last part of the sentence is very often left out when giving a negative answer or negative opinion in order to show the speaker's reluctance. For instance, when asked if a certain day is convenient, one will say

*Sono hi-wa doomo . . .*

This literally means "That day somehow . . . ," but actually conveys the meaning that the day is inconvenient for one.

As *doomo* is very often used to show reluctance or negative judgment, the part following it can be left out, as in:

28

A: *Kono-goro doo-desu-ka.* (How are you these days?)

B: *I-no guai-ga doomo* ... (My stomach is not very good.)

Or, if someone says, while looking at a project plan

*Hiyoo-no ten-de doomo* ...

it means that he cannot approve it in terms of the cost.

The word *chotto* (a little bit) is also used in the same way, as in

*Ano-hito-wa shigoto-wa yoku suru-kedo, hitogara-ga chotto* ... (He is capable at work, but I don't quite like his personality.)

And by using a hesitant, dangling tone, one can convey the same implication without even using such words as *doomo* and *chotto.*

*Sono-hi-wa* ...

*Ano-hito-wa shigoto-wa yoku suru-kedo, hitogara-ga* ...

A negative statement is often understood and left out after *kedo* or *ga* as well. Customers not satisfied with the merchandise shown them by the storekeeper will say something like

*Kore-mo kekkoo-desu-kedo/ga* ... (This is all right, but . . .)

leaving out a phrase meaning "I'd like to see something better/cheaper."

**words implying the continuance of the statement** Words such as *kara, node, kedo,* and *ga* are used to imply that a statement is going to be continued or to ask the listener to continue. There are some other words used in this way.

One is *shi* (and). This is used to connect two or more phrases of similar meaning. For instance,

*Uchi-wa semai-shi, kazoku-ga ooi-shi* ... (My house is small, and I have a large family and . . .)

29

implies that the speaker cannot agree to a visitor staying overnight. *Tari* is also used in this way. For instance, saying

> *Yoru osoku-made ookina koe-de shabettari, terebi-o tsukete-itari-shite* . . . (He talks loudly until late at night, has the television on, and . . .)

implies that the speaker is complaining about a neighbor.

## (4) Sounding hesitant

**a hesitant tone**    Expressing one's reserve by sounding hesitant is essential to being polite, perhaps even more so than using polite expressions. Sounding hesitant means that the speaker proceeds with his or her speech while waiting for the listener's reactions rather than going on without paying any heed to the listener's feelings. This hesitant tone is very important in polite communication; it is used when addressing others, making requests, giving one's own opinion, or making a negative response or evaluation. Namely, it is used when one should show consideration for the listener's feelings.

**when addressing someone**    When addressing someone, one uses such expressions as *anoo*, *moshimoshi*, and *chotto* as well as personal names or the position of the person.

Of the above expressions, *anoo* is the most commonly used. When pronounced with a dangling tone it shows reserve. When it is shortened to *ano* and followed by *ne* as in

> *Ano-ne!*

it sounds familiar.

*Moshimoshi* is used to attract the attention of a stranger as well as to address someone on the telephone. Thus, when calling out to customers who have forgotten their change, a storekeeper will say

> *Moshimoshi, otsuri-desu-yo.* (Hey, you left your change.)

*Chotto* in this sort of situation is familiar and can be rude.

When the other person's name is known to them, the Japanese will address them by name rather than by the second-person pronoun, as in

*Yamada-san!*

*Yoshiko-san!*

Position names are also used in this way:

*Shachoo!* (Company director)

*Okyakusan!* (Customer)

**when making requests** Polite preliminary expressions are usually used when making requests; some examples are

*Sumimasen-ga* ... (I'm sorry but . . .)

*Oisogashii tokoro sumimasen-ga* ... (I'm sorry to trouble you when you're busy.)

*Otesuu-o kakemasu-ga* ... (I'm sorry to trouble you.)

These remarks are good to use, but they have to be said with the right tone. It is best to pause after such a remark and wait for the other person to respond before proceeding on to make your request. Thus, when going to someone working to ask for help, one should talk in the following way to be polite.

A: *Anoo* ...
B: *Hai.*
A: *Oisogashii tokoro sumimasen-ga* ...
B: *Iie, kamaimasen-yo.* (No, that's all right.)
A: *Kore-desu-ga* ... (It's about this.)

This type of hesitant talk is preferred to speaking in one breath like

A: *Ano, oisogashii tokoro sumimasen-ga, kore chotto oshiete-kudasai.*

This means that to be merely verbally fluent is not desirable in terms of politeness when making requests.

**requests and demands**  A hesitant tone implies that the speaker feels that he or she is asking for a special favor from the other person rather than demanding something that is their right. To be polite, it is regarded as good to ask for something as a special favor even when it is well within one's rights. For instance, taking a day off or leaving work early to a certain extent can be regarded as perfectly legitimate nowadays if it causes no inconvenience, but it is still regarded as better to sound hesitant when exercising such a right.

Thus, it is usually considered to be good to talk in the following way:

A: *Kachoo.* (Section chief!)
B: *Un.*
A: *Oisogashii tokoro, chotto sumimasen-ga* . . .
B: *Iya, ii-yo.*
A: *Jitsu-wa kodomo-ga netsu-o dashimashite* . . . (As a matter of fact, my child has a fever.)
B: *Sore-wa ikenai-ne.* (That's too bad.)
A: *Kanai-wa shutchoo-chuu-desu-node* . . . (My wife is on a business trip.)
B: *Soo. Sore-ja* . . . (Is that so? Then . . .)
A: *Shigoto-no hoo-wa kiri-ga tsukimashita-node, dekireba sukoshi hayaku* . . . (The urgent portions of my work have been finished, so if it's possible . . .)
B: *Aa, ii-yo. Hayaku kaerinasai.* (All right. Go home early.)

It would not sound reserved if one talked without pause as in:

A: *Kachoo, oisogashii tokoro chotto sumimasen-ga, jitsu-wa kodomo-ga netsu-o dashimashite, kanai-wa shutchoo-chuu-desu-node, shigoto-no hoo-wa kiri-ga tsukimashita-kara dekireba sukoshi hayaku kaeritai-no-desu-ga.*

**when expressing one's opinion** In polite situations one also tries to sound hesitant when giving an opinion. Usually one starts with

*Soo-desu-nee* . . . (Well — said in a dangling tone)

and then proceeds to give one's opinion. One should not sound too ready to express oneself in a polite situation.

## (5) Sounding indirect

**indirectness** Another important factor when talking politely is to sound indirect. There are two ways of sounding more indirect: one is using indirect expressions such as "*gurai/hodo/bakari*" (about), "*demo*" (or something like that) and "*kamo shiremasen*" (may), and the other is suggesting one's point rather than stating it directly.

**approximate numbers** In social situations the Japanese like to refer to numbers or amounts in a nonspecific way. For instance, when buying apples they will often say

*Mittsu-hodo/gurai/bakari kudasai.* (Please give me about three of them.)

instead of saying

*Mittsu kudasai.*

Or, when suggesting a date to meet, they often say

*Ashita-atari doo-desu-ka.* (How about around tomorrow?)

instead of saying

*Ashita-wa doo-desu-ka.*

33

Especially when asking a favor, they frequently use such expressions as:

*Ichiman-en-bakari kashite-itadakemasen-ka.* (Would you lend me about 10,000 yen?)

English-speaking people also use such expressions as "about twenty," "a few" or "several," but it seems to many Westerners that the Japanese overuse such expressions and dislike giving exact numbers.

The use of such expressions as "*hodo*," "*gurai*," and "*bakari*" shows that the speaker does not want to press the listener by demanding an exact amount. Rather one wants to make the listener comfortable by leaving some margin for choice.

**indirect reference** You may also have noticed that the Japanese tend to refer to things with indirect expressions like "*demo*" and "*nado*" (and others). These expressions are used mainly when offering proposals or suggestions:

*Ocha-demo nomimasen-ka.* (How about having some tea?)

*Eega-demo mimashoo-ka.* (How about going to a movie?)

A: *Mada jikan-ga aru-n-desu-kedo.* (I have some time to kill.)

B: *Ja, zasshi-demo yondara doo-desu-ka.* (Then why don't you read a magazine or something?)

In such situations, "*ocha-demo*" or "*eega-demo*" are preferred to "*ocha-o*" or "*eega-o*" because they let the listener choose among several possibilities. One can order coffee or coke instead of tea at a coffee shop when you have said "*ocha-demo*" instead of "*ocha-o*."

"*Nado*" or "*nanka*" (more familiar) are used when suggesting a possibility, as in:

34

A: *Kono shigoto, dare-ni tanomimashoo-kane.* (Whom shall we ask to do this?)

B: *Yamamoto-san-nanka doo-desu-ka.* (How about Mr. Yamamoto?)

Or, a shopkeeper will say while showing merchandise:

*Kore-nado ikaga-deshoo.* (How do you like this?)

**the indirect development of a discussion**  Similarly, an indirect development is preferred when making a request. Suppose A has made an appointment to meet B at some time in the future but now wants to postpone this. He will talk with B in this way.

A: *Jitsu-wa Kyuushuu-kara tomodachi-ga kuru koto-ni narimashite.* (As a matter of fact, a friend of mine is coming from Kyushu.)

B: *Soo-desu-ka.* (Is that so?)

A: *Tookyoo-wa hajimete-nande.* (This is his first visit to Tokyo.)

B: *Ee.* (Yes.)

A: *Haneda-made itte-yaranai-to . . .* (I'm afraid I have to go to the airport to meet him.)

B: *Taihen-desu-ne.* (That's a lot of trouble, isn't it?)

A: *Ee, maa. Sore-ga mazui koto-ni raigetsu-no tooka-deshite . . .* (Sort of. And that's unfortunately the 10th of next month.)

B: *Aa, soo-desu-ka.* (Oh, really?)

A: *De, dekireba kondo-no yakusoku-o chotto nobashite-itadakitai-n-desu-ga.* (So, I wonder if we could postpone our meeting.)

This may seem very indirect and time-consuming. Not everybody proceeds this way every time, but this is the usual course in a reserved talk. And very often the listener, in this case B, will sense

35

what the other wants before the request is actually made.

**responding to an implicit message** The speaker thus often makes indirect requests, and the listener also responds to implicit messages: this makes the indirect development of speech possible. For instance, a man, usually a superior, will come into the room and say

*Kyoo-wa iya-ni atsui-nee.* (It's awfully hot today, isn't it?)

And one of his men will say "*hai,*" and hurry to open the window or turn on the air conditioner. He may even apologize saying

*Doomo ki-ga tsukimasen-de . . .* (I'm sorry I didn't notice.)

Some people will directly ask to have the window opened, but some people habitually express their requests indirectly and others will do so on occasion. Such indirect requests can be understood best between good friends or family members. Two people who have shared the same experiences can understand each other's wishes without clearly indicating them; the other person will understand what is wanted through an indirect hint or a very short reference to it. And many Japanese seem to find pleasure in being with someone who understands them very well and so will sense their wishes and act to realize them without being asked.

**self-directed statements** Sometimes the Japanese will use self-directed statements to implicitly convey a request. For instance, when one telephones someone and finds he is out, one may say

*Soo-desu-ka. Komatta-na.* (Is that right? What should I do?)

"*Komatta-na*" literally means "I'm troubled." This expression is directed to the speaker rather than to the listener. The listener can choose whether to ignore this or to offer to help in contacting the person as soon as possible.

Not only requests but also complaints are often expressed in this

36

way, although some people prefer direct remarks. A husband may say after tasting his coffee

*Nurui-na.* (It's lukewarm.)

and it is likely that his wife will offer to warm it on her own accord.

## 2. What to Talk About and What Not to Talk About

### (1) Apology and gratitude

**apologetic expressions of gratitude**     Among the various expressions of gratitude used daily are several that may seem to be ones of apology rather than gratitude. In Japanese, gratitude is closely related with apology for having caused trouble to others.

**Sumimasen**     "*Sumimasen*" is used not only to mean "I'm sorry," but also where an English-speaker would say "Thank you." For instance, when a visitor hands a gift such as fruits or candies to the host or hostess, "*Sumimasen*" rather than "*Arigatoo-gozaimasu*" is often used in response.

When receiving a gift a child will say "*Doomo arigatoo*" and between good friends one says "*Arigatoo*" when receiving a gift or some act of kindness, but when one has to be polite one often uses "*Sumimasen.*"

"*Sumimasen*" is used to express gratitude when one didn't expect the act in question or when one feels one should not expect it. In such cases it is regarded as more polite to apologize for having caused so much trouble than to simply thank the other. There is some difference in usage according to generation and between men and women (women are more likely to use "*Sumimasen*" than men), but in general apologetic-sounding expressions are often used as polite expressions of gratitude.

**Ojama-shimashita**     When leaving their host/ess English-

37

speaking persons will express their gratitude for a pleasant time, but in the Japanese custom people usually apologize for taking up the time of the host/ess. Such expressions as

> *Ojama-(ita)shimashita.* (*lit.* I'm sorry I disturbed you.)
>
> *Ojikan-o torimashite* . . . (I'm sorry I took your time.)
>
> *Nagai-o itashimashite* . . . (I'm sorry I took your time — *lit.* I stayed longer than I should have.)

are used together with such expressions of gratitude as

> *Gochisoosama-deshita.* (Thank you very much — *lit.* Thank you for the food.)

It is possible to say something like "*Tanoshikatta-desu*" (It was fun) between good friends, but in polite situations such expressions are not commonly used.

On the part of the host/ess also, instead of thanking the visitor for visiting, he or she will often apologize for not being able to entertain a guest well enough, saying

> *Nanno okamai-mo dekimasen-de, shitsuree-itashimashita.* (I'm sorry I couldn't do anything to entertain you.)

**when meeting again**   When meeting someone again after some time has passed, it is customary to refer to your previous meeting. This is to confirm the good relations between you by recalling a shared experience. In this case too, instead of saying something meaning "We had a wonderful time together," one says

> *Senjitsu-wa shitsuree-itashimashita.* (*lit.* I was rude the other day.)

**expressing gratitude for favors done for family members**   It is customary to say something like

> *Shujin-ga osewa-ni natte-orimasu.*

38

when introduced to an acquaintance of one's family members. This can be literally translated as "My husband is always taken care of by you," but actually means "Thank you for your kindness to my husband." Just as a wife says this, a husband says

*Kanai-ga osewa-ni natte-orimasu.* (My wife . . .)

and parents say

*Kodomo-ga osewa-ni natte-orimasu.* (My child . . .)

or they mention the name of their child such as

*Kazuo-ga osewa-ni natte-orimasu.*

Parents use this expression without fail toward their child's teacher or doctor.

As is true with other expressions, this expression too can be used simply as a formality. A wife may say "*Shujin-ga osewa-ni natte-orimasu*" when she is really grateful as well as when she feels that the listener does not particularly deserve her gratitude.

**identifying oneself with one's family members** We can see two important underlying ideas behind this custom of thanking others for favors done for one's family members. One is that the Japanese feel it essential to express their gratitude for favors done for their family members just as if they had received them themselves. And secondly, since one identifies oneself with one's family members, naturally one also apologizes for the faults of one's family members. For instance, if a boy plays some trick on a neighbor, his parents will apologize as if they had done it themselves. This custom is observed even after one's son or daughter has grown up. It is important in daily life for a parent to express gratitude for the favors done for sons and daughters who have grown up; sometimes a parent will even try to atone for a son's crime by committing suicide.

**thanking for association** Another Japanese idea is that the state of being associated with someone should be regarded as

39

"*osewa-ni naru*" (to be taken care of) because one may be receiving favors from the other even if one doesn't realize it at the time.
Company employees will usually say

*Itsumo osewa-ni natte-orimasu.*

when meeting someone from another company with which their company has transactions. This is similar to the English expression "Thank you for your patronage," but the Japanese seem to extend this custom into a much broader range of usage. This expression of gratitude is used not only between two business organizations but also between nonprofit-making groups.

**okagesama-de**   This attitude of thanking others regardless of whether one realizes some direct factor or not is seen in the use of the expression "*Okagesama-de.*" This expression is used to express gratitude not only for a particular service but also for all that may have been helpful. Thus, one will say to one's doctor

*Okagesama-de yoku narimashita.* (Thanks to you I've recovered.)

And also when an acquaintance asks how one is feeling, the response is

*Okagesama-de yoku narimashita.*

This does not mean that the acquaintance has helped one recover from illness; it means that one feels grateful for all the factors that have made that recovery possible, including the acquaintance. The same underlying idea is seen in such simple daily exchanges as

A: *Ogenki-desu-ka.* (How are you? — *lit.* Are you well?)
B: *Okagesama-de.* (Fine, thank you.)

and

A: *Oshigoto-wa doo-desu-ka.* (How's your work?)
B: *Okagesama-de.* (Thank you. It's going well.)

40

## (2) The taking of blame

**blaming oneself** Being ready to apologize is highly regarded. It is a matter of course to apologize when one is obviously responsible for something; one will immediately apologize when one has accidentally stepped on someone's foot, for instance. But when something has happened and it is not clear who is responsible for it, in Japan it has traditionally been regarded as polite to blame oneself. For instance, when one has borrowed something, a camera, for instance, from one's neighbor and something has gone wrong with it, both the owner and the borrower will readily take the blame for this. Namely, the borrower will say

Kowashimashita. (I broke it.)

as if this had been an intentional act. And the owner will say that it had been in poor condition and apologize for lending such a defective machine.

In fact, this kind of accident requires some sort of settlement; very often a monetary settlement is made. In the case of the camera mentioned above, the borrower will eventually take it to a camera shop and have it fixed, and the cost will be divided between the owner and the borrower. Of course sometimes the borrower just has it fixed without telling the owner anything about it.

As seen in this example, saying "That's my fault" does not necessarily make one responsible for monetary compensation.

The Japanese may seem to be constantly apologizing. They will say "Su(m)imasen" both when inconveniencing others and when receiving favors. Not only that, they are ready to put the blame on themselves in many cases. To give two more examples, when someone finds another person's handwriting difficult to read, the writer will readily apologize for having poor handwriting, and the reader will apologize for being a poor reader. Or, when two people have somehow waited for each other in the wrong place and so couldn't meet at the appointed time, it is polite for both of them to apologize saying that they must have misunderstood.

**variant ways of thinking**    In this way, traditionally it has been regarded as good to put the blame on oneself, and apologies have been accepted with good will. Once a taxi driver took an American woman to a theater, but somehow they arrived at the wrong theater. The woman apologized saying that she must have pronounced the name of the theater wrong. The driver was so pleased by this that he took her to the theater she wanted to go to free of charge.

But this is an exceptionally happy case. This can happen only when both sides hold to the same ideas of politeness. If one side acts this way and the other side does not, the results may be tragic.

One of our American acquaintances had the opposite experience. She borrowed a kerosene heater from her landlady, and something went wrong with it; she went to the landlady and said

*Kowaremashita.* (It broke.)

The landlady looked offended, and their relations were seriously damaged after that. The landlady must have expected the American woman to say

*Kowashite-shimatte, sumimasen.* (I'm sorry I broke it.)

even though she did not intend to ask her to pay for repairs.

Similar misunderstandings often happen, not only between foreigners and the Japanese but also among the Japanese themselves; young people often disregard this idea while older generations value it highly.

This is an issue about which it is difficult to generalize in present-day Japanese society but the following can be said. When two people do not know each other well, they should refrain from saying ''I am to blame'' in cases where material responsibility is involved. You should, however, be ready to apologize to someone whom you know well and who would not charge you simply for apologizing. At the same time you are advised not to expect Japanese who have verbally apologized to always be ready to take monetary respon-

42

sibility. And it is important that you do not regard them as liars; they are only acting in accordance with traditional Japanese ideas of politeness.

## (3) Holding back (not putting oneself forward)

**belittling gifts** Politeness requires the Japanese to make some statement belittling the gifts they are offering to others, as in

>*Makoto-ni tsumaranai mono-desu-ga.* (This is very small.)

>*Okuchi-ni awanai-kamo shiremasen-ga.* (*lit.* It may not suit your palate.)

among various other expressions. Sometimes the gift may be a fine, expensive one, and saying "*tsumaranai mono*" may sound false, but it is nevertheless regarded as good to downplay one's gifts. One should never assume that one's gift is good enough to please the other.

This attitude of depreciating oneself is considered to be polite, and it is seen not only when offering gifts but also when talking about one's abilities or wishes.

**depreciating ability** Except among good friends, the Japanese usually deny any praise received from others. They will never accept a compliment without saying "*Iie.*" To deny praise of one's skills or abilities, one will say

>*Iie, madamada-desu.* (No, I'm not any good at it yet — *lit.* No, not yet.)

>*Iie, watashi-nanka dame-desu.* (Oh, I'm so poor at it — *lit.* Such a person as me is no good.)

When one has to acknowledge praise to some extent, one will say things like:

>*Maa, nantoka.* (I manage to do it somehow.)

>*Okagesama-de nantoka.* (Thanks to everybody I could manage.)

*Doo-yara koo-yara.* (Somehow or other I can do it.)

**demonstrating weakness** Sometimes people purposely complain about their own abilities, saying something like

*Doomo umaku ikanai.* (Somehow it doesn't go well.)

*Doomo umaku dekinai.* (Somehow I just can't do it well.)

This is often seen among the senior persons of a group, those who are trusted and looked up to by younger persons. These people often complain by saying things like

*Kono-goro doomo wasureppoku natte komaru.* (These days I forget things so often.)

*Doomo atama-ga warui mon-da-kara.* (I am so slow to understand things.)

The underlying idea is that influential persons should act so as to conceal their power and put their weaker associates at ease. It is generally regarded as good and even considerate for influential persons to occasionally show their weaknesses. Needless to say, such weaknesses should not be vital ones, but it is better to have some weaknesses than to be perfectly strong and consequently overly powerful or intimidating.

**refraining from expressing convenience** It often happens that when one Japanese asks another what day would be convenient for their next meeting, he answers

*Itsu-demo ii-desu.* (Any time wll do.)

but when they finally come to decide on the date, he says

*Sono hi-wa chotto doomo . . .* (That day won't do — *lit.* As for that day, it's a little . . .)

Or when asked what food he would like to be treated to, he will first say

44

*Nan-demo ii-desu.* (Anything will do.)

first, but actually he can't eat pork, can't eat beef, and can't eat spicy dishes, etc., and he wants nothing but *sashimi*.

Although it would certainly save time and trouble to clearly say what day would be inconvenient or what one cannot eat from the outset, many Japanese think it better not to do so. If the proposed time or choice suits them, that's fine; if it doesn't, then they can show hesitation by saying

$\sim$ *wa chotto* . . .

and wait for another proposal, which will immediately be forthcoming. The underlying idea behind this procedure is that it is not good manners to force others to consider one's own personal convenience.

## (4) Compliments and evaluation

**refraining from direct praise**　　It is usual for people to say nice things to others in social situations; a visitor will compliment the host and hostess on their house or family. It is common to say such things as

*Ii osumai-desu-ne.* (You have a very nice home.)

*Kawaii okosan-desu-ne.* (She is a lovely child.)

But in social situations the Japanese usually refrain from directly praising someone else's looks, abilities or skills. One can praise a child's painting or composition saying

*Joozu-desu-ne.* (Very well done.)

but one cannot use this expression to refer to works done by an adult to whom one has to speak politely.

Most people refrain from directly evaluating their superiors either negatively or positively. They are careful to choose the proper occasion and the appropriate form of expression for such evaluation. In a familiar, friendly atmosphere one can be more free in evaluating one's superiors than in a serious or formal situation.

**benkyoo-ni narimashita** When one wants to praise one's superior on a serious occasion, one has to be careful to choose indirect, subtle expressions. One way to praise a superior's work or achievement is to express gratitude by saying

> *Taihen benkyoo-ni narimashita.* (I learned a great deal from it — *lit.* It became a good study.)

> *Taihen tame-ni narimashita.* (It taught me a great deal — *lit.* It did me a lot of good.)

Expressions of gratitude are felt to be more polite than compliments. When visiting or meeting others, it is all right to compliment them on their house or family, but this does not take the place of expressions of gratitude such as

> *Kanai-ga osewa-ni natte-orimasu.* (Thank you for your kindness to my wife.)

**compliments on the Japanese of foreigners** Many foreigners feel irritated when the Japanese praise their ability to speak Japanese saying

> *Nihongo-ga ojoozu-desu-ne.* (You speak Japanese very well.)

even when they have said just a few simple phrases. This may seem to show that some Japanese do not really take foreigners seriously, but there are other factors at work behind this phenomenon.

One is that the Japanese are not used to talking with those not belonging to the same group and it requires some effort for them to speak to a foreigner. In trying to step outside of their own group and approach a foreigner, they sometimes ask certain questions like "Where are you from?" or "How do you like Japanese food?" And they also give compliments on how well the foreigner

46

speaks Japanese. These questions and compliments are used as a kind of conversation opener.

Another factor is that they are really impressed by a foreigner speaking Japanese since they think it must be very difficult to learn. They are so impressed and even grateful for the foreigner's effort that they forget their sense of politeness that prohibits them from directly praising someone.

On the whole, the fact that many Japanese readily praise foreigners in this way does not mean that it is polite to directly evaluate someone's abilities.

**evaluation and judgment**     It is not polite in Japan to indicate any evaluation or judgment of someone whom one should show respect toward. Therefore it is impolite to say

*Gokuroosama.* (Thank you for your trouble.)

when expressing appreciation for someone's help, because "*Gokuroosama*" implies the speaker's evaluation of the other's hard work. A teacher can say this to his or her students but a student cannot use this expression toward a teacher. This is most often used to thank people for such services as having delivered something or going on an errand; it is most often used toward newspaper boys, porters, deliverymen and the like. Nowadays some people prefer other expressions like "*Arigatoo*" or "*Osewasama*" (Thank you for your help) to "*Gokuroosama*" even in these situations.

The idea that judging someone is impolite explains one difference between "*Hai*" and "*Soo-desu.*" "*Soo-desu*" means "That's right" and is used to express the speaker's agreement. It is all right to use it when indicating agreement to a factual question, as in

A:   *Tanaka-san-desu-ka.* (Are you Mr. Tanaka?)
B:   *Soo-desu.* (That's right.)

47

But when one has to be respectful, it is better to say "*Hai*" rather than "*Soo-desu*" even when indicating agreement. Thus "*Hai*" and "*Soo-desu*" are used together for a polite answer, as in

A: *Tanaka-san-desu-ka.* (Are you Mr. Tanaka?)

B: *Hai, soo-desu.* (Yes, sir/ma'am.)

The expression "*Hai*" does not only indicate agreement but also conveys the speaker's polite attitude or willingness to cooperate with or obey the other person. Thus "*Hai, soo-desu*" can be paraphrased as "I'm going to answer your question politely; the answer is 'yes'."

The underlying idea is that expressing one's agreement directly with "*Soo-desu*" implies that one is going ahead and evaluating or judging the other person, while saying "*Hai*" demonstrates one's polite attitude.

**asking someone's wishes** Asking someone's wishes directly is also impolite in Japan. Saying things like

*Nani-o tabetai-desu-ka.* (What do you want to eat?)

*Nani-ga hoshii-desu-ka.* (What do you want to have?)

should be limited to one's family or close friends. In such a familiar conversation, " ~ *desu-ka*" is not actually used; instead, familiar expressions like

*Nani tabetai?*

*Nani-ga hoshii?*

are natural.

To be polite, one should ask for instructions rather than directly inquire into someone's wishes. Thus, saying

*Mado-o akemashoo-ka.* (Shall I open the window?)

is more appropriate than

*Mado-o akete-moraitai-desu-ka. (Would you like me to open the window?)

When conveying someone's wishes, too, it is best to be indirect. Namely, one should not say something like

*Shachoo-wa ocha-o nomitagatte-irasshaimasu. (The director wants to have some tea.)

Although the polite expression "irasshaimasu" is used in this sentence, directly referring to the director's wishes is not considered to be polite. Instead, one should say something like

Shachoo-ga ocha-o meshiagarimasu. (The director will have some tea.)

## (5) Explanation and discussion

**less explanation and more apology**    Foreign speakers of Japanese sometimes seem impolite because they tend to explain things too much. Especially when making a request or offering an apology, some foreigners will explain their situation or the reason why they are making the request more fully than is expected by the Japanese listener. For instance, when they came late for an appointment, they are apt to explain the reason at length. The Japanese will also give some reason for being late, but it is regarded as good to apologize first, as in

Osoku natte sumimasen. (I'm sorry I'm late.)

and to make the explanation as short as possible. Sometimes they do not offer any explanation at all, but just repeat their apologies.

When offering an explanation, too, one should do so in a reserved way — looking ashamed or guilty, even if the cause was beyond one's responsibility.

Densha-ga okuremashite ... (The train was late.)

is all right, but using "kara" as in

49

> *Densha-ga okuremashita-kara.* (Because the train was late.)

is impolite because it sounds as if one's being late is amply justified and one has no need to feel sorry.

At the very least, the apology should take more time than the explanation in order to be polite.

**when making a request** When making a request too, it is not polite to go on explaining one's reasons without being asked to. And when giving an explanation, one should avoid sounding as if one is not responsible for this. For instance, when asking for an extension of the deadline for a certain job, it is all right to say that the work is taking more time than expected as in

> *Omotta-yori jikan-ga kakarimashite . . .* (It is taking more time than I first thought it would.)

But one should try to avoid sounding as if one is blaming the person who planned it. One often adds another reason such as

> *Doomo shigoto-ga osoi-node . .* (I am not quick at work.)

In such cases such remarks are not to be taken literally. And in making requests, one also refrains from giving too much explanation without being asked.

**"rikutsu" — mere logic** This low evaluation of explanation can be attributed to the fact that the Japanese have long lived in a family-like society and have not frequently confronted the necessity of explanation. Between family members it is regarded as best to understand each other without discussing things, at least in traditional Japanese thinking. When children grow up and try to explain their standpoint, parents, especially the father, tend to scold them by saying

> *Rikutsu-o yuu-na.* (Don't talk back — *lit.* Don't talk about mere logic.)

50

or complain about this saying

> *Rikutsu-bakari iimasu.* (He/She talks nothing but mere logic.)

Many parents think that parents and children should understand each other without depending on verbal explanation, and don't like to discuss things with their children as if they were strangers. They are irritated to hear their children's explanations because they feel that the ideal parent-child relationship is in jeopardy.

This is also seen to some extent in social situations. Many bosses feel offended at having to listen to the unnecessary discussion of their workers. They can't say *"Rikutsu-o yuu-na"* directly to them but they are not happy about having to work with youngsters who talk nothing but *"rikutsu."*

**when offering information** It is in fact rather difficult to make explanations in social situations. The explanation should be sufficient and yet not be overdone. It is impolite to give more explanation than necessary because it implies that one thinks the listener is ignorant. But checking the extent of the other's knowledge is difficult when one has to be polite. This is especially true when the explanation concerns a field the listener feels he knows. Asking with direct expressions such as

> *\*Shitte-imasu-ka.* (Do you know?)

> *\*Gozonji-desu-ka.* (Do you know? — more respectful)

is also impolite when it concerns the listener's intelligence or professional knowledge.

One device to avoid sounding impolite is to use phrases meaning "as you know," such as

> *gozonji-no yoo-ni* (as you know)

> *gozonji-to omoimasu-ga* (I think you know it already but)

Another device is to wait for the listener to express a desire to hear more explanation by saying something like

> *Iya, shiranai-ne. Donnano?* (No, I don't know. What is it like?)

> *Sore-de . . .?* (So . . .?)

## 3.  The Nonverbal Expression of Politeness

### (1) Verbal and nonverbal politeness

**the importance of body language**   There is a common belief that the Japanese use very little body language while speaking, but this is not true. Although they do not use large gestures such as waving their arms or shrugging their shoulders, appropriate body language is regarded as very important in terms of politeness. The wrong use of body language can cause misunderstanding, and may be regarded as impolite.

To be polite in Japanese, the appropriate nonverbal behavior must be used together with verbal expressions. Some expressions must be accompanied by a certain type of body language. For instance, an apology must be offered with a bow, as will be explained shortly. And when offering tea or something to eat, one usually bends one's body and stretches one's right hand toward the other person while saying

> *Doozo meshiagatte-kudasai.* (Please have some.)

Very often "*meshiagatte-kudasai*" is left out and just "*Doozo*" is said. In some situations "*Doozo*" plus the appropriate body language is used without specifically referring to the action in words. Namely, when asking someone to go ahead into a room or an elevator, or to take a seat, "*Doozo*" is often used without adding such phrases as

52

... *ohairi-kudasai.* (please enter the room)

... *okake-kudasai.* (please sit down)

In this way body language both reinforces and supplements polite spoken language.

**body language replacing spoken language** Sometimes body language does not only supplement spoken language but in fact replaces it. For instance, when two people meet on the street or in a building they exchange such expressions as

*Konnichiwa.* (Good day.)

*Ohayoo-gozaimasu.* (Good morning.)

These expressions are often said accompanied by bowing and sometimes a smile. And sometimes just bowing is regarded as sufficient.

In some countries the smile is regarded as most important, and in others verbal expressions are most important, but in Japanese-speaking society bowing is regarded as most important in terms of politeness. It is better to bow without saying anything than to say something polite without bowing. If a young worker or a student raised his hand and said "*Ohayoo-gozaimasu*" with a smile to his boss or professor, he would be regarded as impolite. Thus bowing is given priority over verbal expressions, and can even replace them.

In the case of *aizuchi* too, nodding often takes the place of verbal expressions. (cf. p. 21) Especially when more than two people are listening and one of them gives verbal *aizuchi,* the others give *aizuchi* by nodding. One also often silently bows to express regret and ask for forgiveness when leaving earlier than others from a party or meeting.

## (2) Bowing

**bowing when apologizing** The Japanese often bow or

53

bend their upper body when apologizing. It is not appropriate to say things like

> Sumimasen. (I'm sorry.)

or

> Mooshiwake arimasen. (I'm very sorry.)

with one's upper body held upright and one's chin up. This is not the way a Japanese would apologize, even to a friend. You do not have to make a deep bow when apologizing for some slight offense, but still it is regarded as best to slightly bend your upper body. Needless to say, one has to bow deeply when apologizing for a serious offense.

**bowing when making a request** When making a request, too, one should bow while saying such expressions as

> Sumimasen-ga . . . (I'm sorry to trouble you.)

> Mooshiwake arimasen-ga . . . (I'm very sorry to trouble you.)

Bowing is very important and eloquent in expressing your regret that you have to bother the other person. Even if the request is well within your rights, you should still bow when making a request.

**bowing when offering things** One also usually bows when offering someone something. When serving tea to someone politely one bows to express one's request that the tea be accepted. It is polite to bow when handing over a present because offering it means asking the other person to accept it. While saying something like

> Tsumaranai mono-desu-ga . . . (This is not much, but plaese accept it — lit. This is a trifling thing, but . . .)

one should bend one's upper body. Some foreigners complain that their Japanese acquaintances do not react as expected when they use this expression. It may have been that the two people were talking in a casual manner and this expression was not appropriate. But often the body language they used was not appropriate. Namely, saying this humble expression with one's body upright and one's chin up is strange.

Similarly, offering sympathy for some misfortune should be accompanied with a bow. In the case of offering condolences to a bereaved person, the set expression

> *Kono tabi-wa tonda koto-de-gozaimashita.* (I'm very sorry to hear it — *lit.* This time it was a terrible thing.)

is said while bowing deeply; one bows so deeply while looking down that this expression is not said clearly to the end. In such cases bowing is as eloquent as, or even more eloquent than, words.

**how to bow**  In bowing to express politeness, one slowly bends one's whole body forward and downward. A quick bow will give an impression of casualness or insincerity; an abrupt bow like a duck finding something to eat will seem childish. It is important to spend the appropriate length of time bowing. For instance, when saying

> *Hajimemashite. Doozo yoroshiku.* (How do you do? Glad to meet you — *lit.* This is the first time. Please be good to me.)

to someone you are meeting for the first time, you should bow either after completing the sentence or while saying it. You are advised to start bowing from the second half of the sentence, namely from "*Doozo yoroshiku,*" and bow long enough to say "*Doozo yoroshiku onegai-shimasu.*" In other words, even when using an abbreviated expression, it is best to bow long enough to complete a sentence.

And one should bow at the same time as the other person does. It is embarrassing to straighten up from bowing long before the other person does. In order to bow in accordance with the other person, one has to observe the other person when one starts bowing. If you have finished bowing and see the other person still bowing, you can add another bow.

Generally speaking, women bow more deeply than men, and a younger person should bow more deeply than an older person. The degree of politeness is proportionate with the depth and length of time with which one bows.

Although people nowadays do not bow as long as they used to do years ago, bowing is still practiced faithfully whenever people want to express politeness.

**bending one's upper body** Although the term "bow" has been used in this section, there are actually two different Japanese terms for this. One is *ojigi,* which refers to bending one's body rather deeply. This is used in formal greetings, serious apologies and formal expressions of gratitude or sympathy. To do *ojigi,* one usually bends one's upper body more than 45 degrees; nowadays people tend to bend about 45 degrees and no more than 90 degrees — bowing deeply is used only on very formal occasions or by very polite people.

On the other hand, one often bends one's upper body slightly, from 10 to 15 degrees — this is called *eshaku,* not *ojigi. Eshaku* is used in casual greetings, meeting or passing by acquaintances, and when a superior answers a younger person's *ojigi.* This is similar to "nodding" used in a phrase like "a nodding acquaintance." The difference from nodding is that in *eshaku* the Japanese bend the whole upper body forward rather than just lowering their head.

The Japanese can be observed using this slight bowing very often — sometimes almost constantly. They usually use it when passing an acquaintance in the street; some people use it before sitting down in a seat on the train or in the theater. *Eshaku* very often takes the place of verbal expressions like "*Shitsuree-shimasu*" (Excuse me) in such cases. It is recommended that you respond with *eshaku* when your Japanese acquaintances use it toward you.

### (3) Speaker-listener distance

**more distance** Japanese usually keep more distance between themselves when they talk than many English-speaking people do, and the distance is greater when the two are speaking politely. The Japanese sometimes feel embarrassed when their American acquaintances come closer to them than they feel appropriate. We know several Americans who have felt offended at seeing their Japanese acquaintances step back from them.

Between good friends the distance left can be very small; the distance is proportionate to the degree of politeness. Students usually do not stand very close to their teachers, and young workers refrain from coming too close to their bosses. And the distance is larger when the two persons are of the opposite sex.

**bowing and shaking hands** The speaker-listener distance varies depending on whether the two people bow or shake hands. When the two are going to bow to each other, they have to stand relatively far apart; otherwise their heads will touch when they bow. On the other hand if the two are going to shake hands, they have to stand closer together. You may have experienced some awkwardness about shaking hands with a Japanese because he was standing too far away. Some Japanese can be seen bowing slightly while shaking hands because they are not standing close enough to the other person.

**the proper distance** It is important to keep an appropriate distance between the speaker and the listener, but standing too far away gives an impression of strangeness. It is difficult to indicate the distance exactly, but you can regard it as safe to stand the distance of your heads when bent deepest plus 15 to 20 centimeters. This means that you can safely bow deeply to each other. Depending on the stature of the persons, the distance is thus from 1.5 meters to 2 meters apart.

### (4) Other examples of polite body language

**handing things to others** When handing something to

57

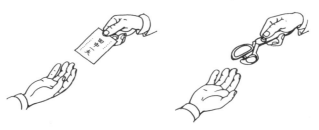

someone, it is polite to hand it so that they can use it as it is, without turning it around. For example, when giving someone your name card, you should do so in a way that the other person can read it without turning it around. This is true in the case of handing over letters, documents and books. If you are handing someone a pair of scissors, you should hand them so that they can be held as they are.

**giving money**   The Japanese take care not to act business-like when giving money to someone for personal help. In schools, for instance, one pays tuition directly to a clerk or through a bank. But when you take personal lessons in such subjects as traditional dance, flower arrangement, calligraphy, and the like, you have to take care so that you do not seem to be too businesslike. You should not hand money as is to your teacher; you should put the money in an envelope and hand it over in an inconspicuous manner — quietly slipping it to the side of the teacher for instance.

Not only in the physical act of handing over money, but also in discussing monetary matters, there is a traditional idea that one should not directly show interest in money, in the case of personal help. When someone is asked to give a special lecture at a meeting of people who are not directly associated with him, for instance, he hesitates to ask how much he will be paid for the lecture. This is because there is an idea that one should not expect to be paid for personal services. In such cases the person who asks someone's help should take care to offer information about the pay so that the other person does not have to directly ask about this.

58

# PART II   VERBAL POLITENESS

## 1. Level of Speech

### (1) Polite speech and familiar speech

**two levels**   In daily conversation two levels of speech, namely, polite speech and familiar speech, are used. Generally speaking, polite speech is used in social situations such as conversations between acquaintances or strangers and familiar speech in familiar conversations between good friends or family members. The two levels are mainly distinguished by different sentence endings and different vocabulary items.

**different sentence endings**   In polite speech sentences usually end in polite forms, namely, "*desu*" and "*-masu.*"

> ACQUAINTANCE A: *Ii otenki-desu-ne.* (Fine day, isn't it?)
> ACQUAINTANCE B: *Ee, soo-desu-ne.* (Yes, isn't it?)
>
> PASSENGER: *Kono basu, Ku-yakusho-mae-ni tomarimasu-ka.* (Does this bus stop at the ward office?)
> BUS DRIVER: *Iie, tomarimasen.* (No, it doesn't.)

In familiar speech, sentences end in plain forms — namely, the dictionary form of adjectives and verbs and "*da*":

> HIGH SCHOOL STUDENT A: *Ashita, eega-ni iku?* (Are you going to the movie tomorrow?)
> HIGH SCHOOL STUDENT B:*Mada wakaranai.* (I don't know yet.)
>
> HUSBAND: *Mata ame-da-ne.* (Rain again!)

59

WIFE: *Moo mikka-me-**da**-wane.* (This is the third day, isn't it?)

**polite forms and plain forms**   The difference between polite forms and plain forms is as follows:

a) verbs

Verbs are used in the "*-masu*" form in polite speech.

Polite: 1. *Ashita ikimasu.* (I'm going tomorrow.)
2. *Ashita-wa ikimasen.* (I'm not going tomorrow.)
3. *Kinoo ikimashita.* (I went yesterday.)
4. *Kinoo-wa ikimasen-deshita.* (I didn't go yesterday.)
5. *Ashita ikimashoo.* (Let's go tomorrow.)

The following are the plain speech counterparts of 1–5:

Plain: 1. *Ashita iku.*
2. *Ashita-wa ikanai.*
3. *Kinoo itta.*
4. *Kinoo-wa ikanakatta.*
5. *Ashita ikoo.*

b) adjectives ending in *-i*

The true adjectives or *-i* adjectives are used with "*desu*" (present), "*deshita*" (past), "*-ku arimasen*" (present negative) and "*-ku arimasen-deshita*" (past negative) in polite speech; they are used without "*desu*" or "*deshita*," and "*deshoo*" is replaced by "*daroo*" in plain speech.

Polite: 1. *Samui-desu.* (It's cold.)
2. *Samuku arimasen.* (It's not cold.)
3. *Samukatta-desu.* (It was cold.)
4. *Samuku arimasen-deshita/Samuku nakatta-desu.* (It wasn't cold.)
5. *Samui-deshoo.* (It must be cold.)

Plain: 1. *Samui.*

60

    2. *Samuku nai.*

    3. *Samukatta.*

    4. *Samuku nakatta.*

    5. *Samui-daroo.*

c) quasi-adjectives

Quasi-adjectives (also known as adjective-verbs or *-na* adjectives) are just like nouns, as far as sentence endings are concerned.

d) noun plus "*desu*" or "*da*"

In polite speech "*desu*" is used with nouns, while "*da*" is used in plain speech.

Polite:  1. *Ii otenki-desu.* (It's a fine day.)

          2. *Ii otenki-ja arimasen.* (It isn't a fine day.)

          3. *Ii otenki-deshita.* (It was a fine day.)

          4. *Ii otenki-ja arimasen-deshita.* (It wasn't a fine day.)

          5. *Ii otenki-deshoo.* (It should be a fine day.)

Plain:  1. *Ii tenki-da.*

        2. *Ii tenki-ja nai.*

        3. *Ii tenki-datta.*

        4. *Ii tenki-ja nakatta.*

        5. *Ii tenki-daroo.*

e) other difference

In polite speech, sentences usually end in "*-masu*" or "*desu*," while in plain speech sometimes just phrases are used.

Polite: A: *Itsu odekake-desu-ka.* (When are you leaving?)

         B: *Ashita dekakemasu.* (I'm leaving tomorrow.)

Plain: A: *Itsu dekakeru?* (When are you leaving?)

       B: *Ashita.* (Tomorrow.)

When speaking politely, one should avoid verbless sentences like

    *Ato-de (kimasu).* (I'll come later.)

61

*Sakki (kimashita). (He came a while ago.)

unless what precedes the verb is a polite expression, as in

Nochi-hodo (mairimasu). (I'll come later.)

Saki-hodo (omie-ni narimashita). (He came a while ago.)

**Sentence particles** There are several particles used at the end of sentences. "Ne" is most frequent as in

Ii otenki-desu-**ne**. (Fine day, isn't it?)

Asoko-ni ginkoo-ga arimasu-**ne**. (There's a bank over there, as you can see.)

It is used either to solicit the listener's agreement or to make sure that the listener has understood. "Yo," on the other hand, is used to emphatically state one's own opinion, as in

Kore-wa totemo ii-desu-**yo**. Zehi tsukatte-mite-kudasai. (This is very good. You should by all means try it.)

These two particles "ne" and "yo" are used both in polite speech and familiar speech. Other sentence particles such as "sa" (casual), "ze" (emphasis on one's opinion), and "zo" (more emphatic than "ze") are used only in familiar speech.

Sentence particles are, however, sometimes used at the end of a phrase as in

Kinoo-**ne**, ginkoo-e ittara-**ne**, Yamamoto-san-ga ite-**ne** . . . (When I went to the bank, I saw Mr. Yamamoto, you know.)

Since using sentence particles in this way creates an impression of familiarity, it is limited to familiar speech. "Ne" is often used in this way in familiar speech, but using "yo" in this way is quite limited because it is regarded as vulgar. This also applies to "sa," "ze" and "zo"; "yo" and these particles should not be used between phrases even in familiar speech.

## (2) The use of plain forms in polite speech

Although plain forms are not used at the end of the sentence in polite speech, they are used when 1) modifying nouns, 2) expressing indirect speech, 3) indicating the speaker's opinion, and 4) in the "*n-desu*" form.

a) noun modifiers

Plain forms are used in phrases modifying nouns. For instance:

*kinoo **katta** hon* (a book which I bought yesterday)

*booshi-o kabutte-**iru** hito* (a person wearing a hat)

Even when used in sentences with polite endings the modifying phrases remain in the plain form:

*Kore-wa kinoo **katta** hon-desu.* (This is a book I bought yesterday.)

*Booshi-o kabutte-**iru** hito-wa Yamada-san desu.* (The man wearing a hat is Mr. Yamada.)

Polite forms in modifying phrases as in

*\*Kore-wa kinoo **kaimashita** hon-desu.*

*\*Booshi-o kabutte-**imasu** hito-wa Yamada-san-desu.*

are understood, but sound strange and foreign.

Not only concrete nouns such as "*hon*" (book) and "*booshi*" (hat), but also abstract nouns such as "*toki*" (time), "*tokoro*" (situation) and "*koto*" (fact) are modified by verbs and adjectives in the plain form:

*Kono tsugi **kuru** toki motte-kimasu.* (I'll bring it when I come next time.)

*Ima **tsuita** tokoro-desu.* (I have just arrived.)

*Mada **mita** koto-ga arimasen.* (I have not seen it before.)

63

As illustrated in the sentences above, words such as *"toki,"* *"tokoro"* and *"koto"* do not have substantial meaning; they are used like conjunctions or particles rather than as nouns. These are called form nouns; there are several other nouns used in a similar way: *"mono,"* *"wake,"* *"kuse,"* *"tame,"* *"see,"* *"hazu"* and so on. To give a few examples:

> *Kaisha-o* **yasumu** *wake-niwa ikimasen.* (I can't very well be absent from the office.)

> *Moo sorosoro* **kuru** *hazu-desu.* (It's about time for him to come.)

> *Shippai-shita-nowa doryoku-ga* **tarinakatta** *see-desu.* (I failed because I did not work hard enough.)

> *Sonna koto-o* **yuu** *mon(o)-ja arimasen.* (You shouldn't say such a thing.)

b) expressing indirect speech

Plain forms are used in indirect speech, as in

1. **Isogashii**-*to itte-imashita.* (He said that he was busy.)

2. *Shigoto-ga* **mitsukatta**-*to itte-imashita.* (She said that she had found a job.)

3. *Omoshiroku* **nai**-*to itte-imashita.* (He said that it wasn't interesting.)

4. *Zannen-***da**-*to itte-imashita.* (She said that she regretted it.)

In the examples above, the person who is quoted may have used polite forms as in

1. *Isogashii-desu.*
2. *Shigoto-ga mitsukarimashita.*
3. *Omoshiroku arimasen.*
4. *Zannen-desu.*

64

But in quoting them, it is appropriate to use plain forms.

In the same way, plain forms are used before such expressions as "*soo-desu*" (I heard), "*to yuu koto-desu*" (I understand), and "*to yuu hanashi-desu*" (they say):

> *Yamada-san-ga **kuru** soo-desu.* (I heard that Mr. Yamada is coming.)

> *Dame-**datta**-to yuu koto-desu.* (I heard that he failed.)

> *Byooki-ga **naotta**-to yuu hanashi-desu.* (I was told that he has recovered from his illness.)

c) expressing one's opinion or judgment

Plain forms are also used before "*to omoimasu*" (I think) as in

> *Sore-ga **ii**-to omoimasu.* (I think that's good.)

> *Zannen-**da**-to omoimashita.* (I felt it was regrettable.)

In the same way, the phrases preceding "*rashii-desu*," "*yoo-desu*," and "*kamo shiremasen*" are in the plain form, as in

> *Yamada-san-ga **yatta**-rashii-desu.* (It seems that Mr. Yamada did it.)

> *Daibu okane-ga **kakaru** yoo-desu.* (It looks like it will cost him a lot.)

> *Dame-**datta**-kamo shiremasen.* (He may have failed.)

d) *n-desu* & *n-da*

Plain forms are used with the patterns "*n-desu*" and "*n-da*"; the former is used in polite speech and the latter in familiar speech.

> ACQUAINTANCE A: *Doo **shita**-n-desu-ka.* (What's the matter?)
> ACQUAINTANCE B: *Chotto onaka-ga **itai**-n-desu.* (I have a slight stomachache.)

65

FRIEND A: *Doo shita-n-da.* (What's the matter?)
FRIEND B: *Chotto onaka-ga itai-n-da.* (I have a slight stomachache.)

i) *n-desu*
The "*n-desu*" endings are made up as follows:
Verbs in the plain form are followed by "*n-desu.*"

1. *Iku-n-desu.* (I am going.)
2. *Itta-n-desu.* (I went.)

Adjectives are followed by "*n-desu*" as in

3. *Oishii-n-desu.* (It is delicious.)
4. *Oishikatta-n-desu.* (It was delicious.)

*-na* adjectives are also followed by "*n-desu.*"

5. *Genkina-n-desu.* (He's well.)
6. *Genki-datta-n-desu.* (He was well.)

Noun-plus-*desu* sentences are changed to:

7. *Ii otenki-na-n-desu.* (The weather is fine.)
8. *Ii otenki-datta-n-desu.* (The weather was fine.)

Those sentences are very close in form to such sentences as:

1. *Ikimasu.*
2. *Ikimashita.*
3. *Oishii-desu.*
4. *Oishikatta-desu.*
5. *Genki-desu.*
6. *Genki-deshita.*
7. *Ii otenki-desu.*
8. *Ii otenki-deshita.*

These two sets of sentences are both used in polite speech, but their function is different.

*"n-desu"* is basically used to explain, or refer to, a certain situation. For instance, saying

> *Byooki-desu.* (He is sick.)

just states someone's condition. But if you say

> *Byookina-n-desu.* (It is that he is sick.)

you are explaining the reason why he cannot come to work or why you are giving him permission to leave early, or the like.

If you ask someone

> *Nemui-desu-ka.*

you are simply asking if he or she is sleepy. But if you say

> *Nemui-n-desu-ka.*

you are implying that the other person looks sleepy or bored or something similar.

Asking someone

> *Kekkon-shite-iru-n-desu-ka.*

instead of

> *Kekkon-shite-imasu-ka.*

can imply something like "Are you anxious to go home so early because you are married and have to have supper with your husband?"

> *Jikan-ga arimasen.*

simply states that you don't have time, but

> *Jikan-ga nai-n-desu.*

is used when you want to decline a request or urge someone to hurry.

If you use this form in asking a question, you will be asking the reason for a certain situation rather than asking for simple information.

Thus you should be careful in using the "*n-desu*" form for questions.

Besides asking or stating the reason for a certain situation, the "*n-desu*" form is used to emphatically state a judgment or emotion. When it is used without referring to any particular situation, it expresses the speaker's strong wish to have the listener understand or sympathize. For instance, saying

> *Honto-ni ano-hito iyana hito-na-n-desu.* (He is really a disagreeable person.)

can mean either that the speaker is giving the reason why he wants to shun the person or that he is simply emphasizing his dislike. Naturally enough, this use sounds emotional, and the overuse of "*n-desu*" should be avoided.

ii) *n-da*

What has been said about "*n-desu*" also applies to "*n-da*," except that the former is used in polite speech while the latter is used in familiar speech. Namely, saying

> *Byooki-na-n-da.*

is used either to explain a certain situation or to emphasize that someone is sick. Also, asking

> *Nemui-no-ka.*

> *Kekkon-shite-iru-no-ka.*

implies that you want to know the reason for a certain situation. (When "*n-da*" precedes the particle "*ka*" signifying a question, "*da*" is dropped and "*n*" changes to "*no.*" In women's speech "*da*" and "*ka*" are usually dropped: *Byooki-na-no, Nemui-no?, Kekkon-shite-iru-no?*)

68

### (3) Politeness and vocabulary

**polite words** It is of course necessary to use polite words when referring to someone else's family or belongings. Polite words are also often used to make the tone of speech more polite when referring to things that do not belong to anybody in particular. For instance, the word *"tenki"* (weather) is often used with *"o,"* the polite prefix, in polite speech, as in

*Ohayoo-gozaimasu. Ii otenki-desu-ne.* (Good morning. Fine day, isn't it?)

In familiar conversation people sometimes add *"o"* and sometimes do not. One can say either

*Ohayoo. Ii tenki-dane.* (men)

or

*Ohayoo. Ii otenki-dane.* (men)
*Ohayoo. Ii otenki-ne.* (women)

Generally speaking, women use *"o"* more often even in familiar speech, but nowadays men's and women's speech are coming closer to each other, and men tend to use *"o"* more often than they did ten or twenty years ago.

**words not used with "o"** Differences in politeness can be observed in words that are closely related to personal relations like family terms and in words frequently used in daily life like words concerning meals. On the other hand, public organizations, public buildings and academic institutions are not referred to with *"o."* For instance, the following words are not used with *"o"*:

*gakkoo* (school)
*byooin* (hospital)
*ginkoo* (bank)
*yuubinkyoku* (post office)
*toshokan* (library)
*eki* (station)

**words concerning personal relations**    One difference between men's speech and women's speech is seen in words concerning personal relations.

|  | Predominantly women's speech | Predominantly men's speech |
|---|---|---|
| baby | akachan | akanboo |
| friend | otomodachi | tomodachi |
| neighbor | otonari | tonari |
| husband | goshujin | teeshu, shujin |
| wife | okusan | saikun, okusan |
| father | otoosan, chichioya | chichioya, oyaji |
| mother | okaasan, hahaoya | hahaoya, ofukuro |

Women often add "o" to such words regardless of whom they refer to. For instance, "o" is not usually added to one's own belongings, but in the case of "tomodachi," women tend to say "otomodachi" even when referring to their own friends.

**words concerning meals**    Since meals are so closely related with everyday life, a wide range is observed in politeness; on the whole polite words are used by women.

|  | Polite speech in general (used by both sexes) | Female polite speech | Male familiar speech | Formal speech |
|---|---|---|---|---|
| meal | shokuji, gohan | oshokuji, gohan | meshi | shokuji |
| breakfast | asagohan, asahan | asagohan | asameshi | chooshoku |
| lunch | ohiru | ohirugohan | hiru, hirumeshi | chuushoku |
| dinner | bangohan, yuuhan | bangohan | banmeshi | yuushoku |
| a snack between meals | oyatsu | oyatsu |  | kanshoku |
| a snack at night | yashoku | oyashoku | yashoku |  |
| tea | ocha | ocha | (o)cha |  |

70

| | | | | |
|---|---|---|---|---|
| alcoholic beverage | *osake* | *osake* | *sake* | |
| sweets | *okashi* | *okashi* | *okashi* | |
| box lunch | *obentoo* | *obentoo* | *(o)bentoo* | *bentoo* |
| to eat | *taberu* | *itadaku* | *kuu* | *toru* |
| to drink | *nomu* | *itadaku* | *nomu* | *toru* |
| delicious | *oishii* | *oishii* | *umai* | |
| cooking pot | *nabe* | *onabe* | *nabe* | |
| rice-cooker | *kama* | *okama* | *kama* | |
| rice bowl | *chawan* | *ochawan* | *chawan* | |
| chopsticks | *hashi* | *ohashi* | *hashi* | |
| plate | *sara* | *osara* | *sara* | |
| fish | *sakana* | *osakana* | *sakana* | |
| meat | *niku* | *oniku* | *niku* | *shokuniku* |
| beef | *gyuuniku* | *gyuuniku* | *gyuuniku* | |
| sushi | *sushi* | *osushi* | *sushi* | |
| soy sauce | *shooyu* | *oshooyu* | *shooyu* | |
| sugar | *satoo* | *osatoo* | *satoo* | |
| salt | *shio* | *oshio* | *shio* | |
| pepper | *koshoo* | *koshoo* | *koshoo* | |
| sauce | *soosu* | *osoosu* | *soosu* | |
| miso soup | *miso-shiru* | *omiso-shiru* | *miso-shiru* | |
| clear soup | *sumashi-jiru, suimono* | *osumashi, osuimono* | *suimono, sumashi-jiru* | |
| onion | *negi* | *onegi* | *negi* | |
| tofu | *toofu* | *otoofu* | *toofu* | |
| pickles | *tsukemono* | *otsukemono, okooko* | *tsukemono, kooko* | |

## other words used in daily life

| | Polite speech in general (used by both sexes) | Female polite speech | Male familiar speech | Formal speech |
|---|---|---|---|---|
| bath | *ofuro* | *ofuro* | *furo* | *nyuuyoku* |
| toilet | *toire, tearai* | *otoire, otearai* | *toire, benjo* | *benjo* |
| money | *okane* | *okane* | *kane* | |
| home | *uchi* | *ouchi* | *uchi* | *jitaku* |
| clothes | *fuku, yoofuku* | *oyoofuku* | *fuku, yoofuku* | *irui* |

(Continued on next page)

71

(Continued from previous page)

| shopping | kaimono | okaimono | kaimono | |
| room | heya | oheya | heya | |
| book | hon | gohon | hon | shomotsu, shoseki |
| studying | benkyoo | obenkyoo | benkyoo | |

Words of foreign origin, such as *"rajio"* (radio) and *"terebi"* (television), are not usually used with *"o,"* but several common words are used with *"o,"* such as *"otoire"* and *"obiiru"* (beer).

Women tend to use *"o"* more often when talking to children, as in

> MOTHER:  *Yoshiko-san,   otete-o   aratte,   obenkyoo-shimashoo-ne.* (Yoshiko, wash your hands and study.)

Some special words are used when talking to very young children: *"otete"* (hand) is one of them.

## (4) Differences between men's and women's speech

**differences in politeness**   Differences in politeness between men's speech and women's speech depend on the situation. There is little difference between men's and women's speech in work situations and in public speaking. A female candidate for the Diet talks just as a male candidate does. In business discussions women talk like men. A woman professor gives her lectures in the same language as a man does. In short, in impersonal polite speech there is very little difference between men's and women's speech.

In personal conversation, however, there are some differences. In polite conversation with their acquaintances, women, especially older women, tend to speak more politely than men; they use polite verbs more often and use some feminine sentence endings. In familiar conversation men's speech differs very much in the sentence endings used. If you read a familiar conversation between a man and a woman in a novel, it is easy to tell what is spoken by the woman and what by the man from the sentence endings.

72

### differences in sentence endings in familiar speech

a) verbs and -i adjectives

Both men and women use the plain form of verbs and -i adjectives.

| MEN | | WOMEN |
|---|---|---|
| *Iku.* | I'm going. | *Iku.* |
| *Itta.* | I went. | *Itta.* |
| *Ikanai.* | I'm not going. | *Ikanai.* |
| *Ikanakatta.* | I didn't go. | *Ikanakatta.* |
| *Oishii.* | It's delicious. | *Oishii.* |
| *Oishikatta.* | It was delicious. | *Oishikatta.* |
| *Oishiku nai.* | It isn't delicious. | *Oishiku nai.* |
| *Oishiku nakatta.* | It wasn't delicious. | *Oishiku nakatta.* |

Women add "*wa*" for mild emphasis.

| | | WOMEN |
|---|---|---|
| | I AM going. | *Iku-**wa**.* |
| | I WENT. | *Itta-**wa**.* |
| | I'm NOT going. | *Ikanai-**wa**.* |
| | I did NOT go. | *Ikanakatta-**wa**.* |
| | It IS delicious. | *Oishii-**wa**.* |
| | It WAS delicious. | *Oishikatta-**wa**.* |
| | It was NOT delicious. | *Oishiku nakatta-**wa**.* |

The particles "*ne*" and "*yo*" are used by both men and women. Women add them to "*wa*."

| MEN | | WOMEN |
|---|---|---|
| *Iku-**ne**.* | I'm going, you know. | *Iku-**wa-ne**.* |
| *Iku-**yo**.* | I'm going, I tell you. | *Iku-**wa-yo**.* |

b) nouns and -na adjectives

"*Desu*" becomes "*da*" in men's familiar speech; in women's familiar speech, it is either omitted or "*da-wa*" is used after nouns and -na adjectives; "*da-wa*" is a little more emphatic.

73

| MEN | | WOMEN |
|---|---|---|
| Ashita-da.<br><br>Kiree-da. | It's tomorrow.<br><br>It's pretty. | Ashita.<br>Ashita-da-wa.<br>Kiree.<br>Kiree-da-wa. |

"*Deshita*" becomes "*datta*" in men's speech and "*datta(-wa)*" in women's.

| MEN | | WOMEN |
|---|---|---|
| Kinoo-datta.<br><br>Kiree-datta. | It was yesterday.<br><br>It was pretty. | Kinoo-datta.<br>Kinoo-datta-wa.<br>Kiree-datta.<br>Kiree-datta-wa. |

The particles "*ne*" and "*yo*" are added to the above; women use "*datta-wa*" before "*ne*" or "*yo*."

| MEN | | WOMEN |
|---|---|---|
| Ashita-da-ne.<br><br>Ashita-da-yo.<br><br>Kinoo-datta-ne.<br>Kinoo-datta-yo. | It's tomorrow, isn't it?<br><br>It's tomorrow, I tell you.<br><br>It was yesterday, wasn't it?<br>It was yesterday, I tell you. | Ashita-ne.<br>Ashita-da-wa-ne.<br>Ashita-yo.<br>Ashita-da-wa-yo.<br>Kinoo-datta-wa-ne.<br>Kinoo-datta-wa-yo. |

c) *n-desu*

"*n-desu*" becomes "*na-n-desu*" after nouns and -*na* adjectives in polite speech, as in "*Genki-na-n-desu*." In familiar speech used by men it becomes "*na-n-da*" and for women "*na-no*."

| MEN | | WOMEN |
|---|---|---|
| Kiree-na-n-da.<br>Ashita-na-n-da. | It is that it is pretty.<br>It is that it is tomorrow. | Kiree-na-no.<br>Ashita-na-no. |

The particles "*ne*" and "*yo*" can also be added.

## LEVEL OF SPEECH

| MEN | | WOMEN |
|---|---|---|
| *Ashita-na-n-da-ne.* | It's that it's tomorrow, isn't it? | *Ashita-na-no-ne.* |
| *Kiree-na-n-da-ne.* | It's that it's pretty, isn't it? | *Kiree-na-no-ne.* |
| *Ashita-na-n-da-yo.* | It's that it's tomorrow, I tell you. | *Ashita-na-no-yo.* |
| *Kiree-na-n-da-yo.* | It's that it's pretty, I tell you. | *Kiree-na-no-yo.* |

d) familiar requests

In polite speech, requests are expressed by such sentence endings as *"te-kudasai,"* *"te-kudasaimasen-ka,"* and *"te-itadakemasen-ka."*

In familiar speech, the pattern *"te-kurenai?"* is used by both men and women, as in

> MEN/WOMEN: *Chotto matte-kurenai?* (Wait a moment, won't you?)

To make this request even shorter, both men and women use *"te"* as in

> MEN/WOMEN: *Chotto matte!* (Wait a moment!)

In this usage women tend to add *"ne"* at the end to soften the tone, as in

> WOMEN: *Warui-kedo, chotto matte-ne.* (Sorry. Wait a moment, would you?)

Men sometimes use this expression when speaking to children or younger people.

e) the expression of probability

*"Deshoo"* becomes *"daroo"* in men's speech, while *"deshoo"* is used in women's speech.

75

| MEN | | WOMEN |
|---|---|---|
| *Iku-daroo.* | He will probably go. | *Iku-deshoo.* |
| *Ikanai-daroo.* | He will probably not go. | *Ikanai-deshoo.* |
| *Itta-daroo.* | He probably went. | *Itta-deshoo.* |
| *Ikanakatta-daroo.* | He probably didn't go. | *Ikanakatta-deshoo.* |
| *Ashita-daroo.* | It is probably tomorrow. | *Ashita-deshoo.* |
| *Kiree-daroo.* | It is probably pretty. | *Kiree-deshoo.* |
| *Kinoo-datta-daroo.* | It was probably yesterday. | *Kinoo-datta-deshoo.* |
| *Kiree-datta-daroo.* | It was probably pretty. | *Kiree-datta-deshoo.* |

"~ *kashira*" (I wonder) is used more often by women, as in

*Kore-de tariru-kashira.* (I wonder if this will be enough.)

*Doko-e itta-no-kashira.* (I wonder where he went.)

On the other hand the ending "*kana*" (I wonder) is usually used by men in familiar speech, as in

*Kore-de tariru-kana.* (I wonder if this will be enough.)

*Doko-e itta-no-kana.* (I wonder where he went.)

The particle "*na*," which is used to express emotion, is used more often by men, as in

*Kore-wa ii-na.* (Oh, this is good!)

*Iya-da-na.* (How disagreeable!)

although women use it when speaking to themselves.

**differences in vocabulary** Women tend to use more polite words than men do, and they also add "*o*" to more words. (See the previous section.)

Besides this, women are allowed to use emotional expressions more freely than men. For instance, although such adjectives as "*suteki*" (marvelous) and "*kawaii*" (cute) are used by both men and women, they are used much more often by women. This means that when a man just praises something by saying "*Ii-ne*" (Good.), a woman may use more emphatic words like "*suteki*" or "*kawaii*."

Some differences can also be seen in the use of interjections. To express their surprise at seeing someone unexpectedly, men will say "*Yaa*" or "*Yaa, kore-wa kore-wa,*" while women will say "*Maa*" or "*Ara!*" ("*maa*" and "*ara*" are never used by men).

This difference is seen in tone, too. Women's voices rise and fall within a greater range than men's when freely expressing feelings.

**men to men, women to women, men to women** When men talk in familiar speech to other men, they tend to become very familiar; they will use such words as "*meshi*" and "*kuu*" in place of "*gohan*" and "*taberu*." On the other hand, when men talk with women, they tend to speak more politely; in other words, when with women, men tend to adopt women's speech. For instance, two male colleagues will talk about going out for lunch as in

> MAN A: *Meshi-ni shiyoo-ka.* (Shall we eat?)
> MAN B: *Un, ikoo.* (Yes, let's.)

Then a woman employee happens to approach the two. They will quickly change tone.

> MAN A: *A, ohiru-ni shinai?* (Shall we have lunch?)
> MAN B: *Un, issho-ni ikanai?* (Why don't you join us?)

On the other hand, women do not change their tone when they talk with men; they usually remain polite.

**adults to children** In adults' speech towards children, a tendency similar to that of men talking to women is seen. When talking to children, adults tend to use a familiar tone and softened sentence endings as in

> MEN/WOMEN: *Kazuko-chan, ouchi-e kaeroo-ne.* (Let's go home, Kazuko.)

> MEN/WOMEN: *Kazuo-chan, gohan-no mae-niwa otete*

77

*araimashoo-ne.* (Let's wash our hands before eating, shall we?)

Adults tend to adopt children's speech. In other words, the one in the stronger position adopts the speech habits of the one in the weaker position. Adults also use this kind of language when they talk to very old and weak people.

## (5) Refined speech — new tendencies

**new tendencies in polite language**     Polite language has undergone many changes in the postwar period, as explained in Part I. Extremely polite expressions have come to be out of favor, and deprecatory or rough-sounding expressions have also come to be used less often. In a word, language in present-day Japan has been simplified in terms of politeness.

Along with this change, minute differences in expressions according to human relations have come to be loosened. For example, different terms for referring to one's own family and to someone else's were strictly observed in traditional usage, and young mothers who refer to their own babies as "*akachan*" (polite) instead of "*akanboo*" (non-polite) are still criticized by people following the traditional usage. Similarly, giving something to someone in one's own family was traditionally referred to by the verb "*yaru*," but nowadays people, especially women, use "*ageru*" which sounds more polite.

This simplification in levels of politeness can be attributed to (1) modernization, (2) diversity in human relationships, and (3) women's advances in society.

**modernization**     Modern ways of thinking, especially in regard to equality and individuality, affect the use of language. Namely, people have come to talk with each other on a more equal basis now, although this may be difficult for foreigners to believe. Compared with prewar Japan customers now speak more politely and storekeepers less politely. In sushi shops, for instance, cooks used to say

> *Nani-o meshiagarimasu-ka.* (What would you like to have? — *"meshiagaru"* is a respectful expression)

> *Nan-ni nasaimasu-ka.* (What would you like to have? — *"nasaru"* is a respectful expression)

but nowadays many cooks say *"Nan-ni shimasu-ka"* to mean the same thing; here no expression of respect is included. The customers used to say just *"maguro"* (tuna) or *"ika"* (squid) bluntly, but nowadays they usually say

> *Maguro kudasai.* (Tuna, please.)

or

> *Ika, tanomimasu.* (Squid, please.)

Along with these changes, people now have a weaker sense of identification with family members as far as language use is concerned. Thus they say *"ageru"* to both family members and to non-family members.

**diversity in human relations**   Japan now accepts more foreigners in its society, and within Japanese society itself social mobility is much higher than before. Many young people come to work in big cities, where they come into contact with various types of people. Before the war, people had far fewer chances to talk with strangers, much less with foreigners, than they do now. An average person in prewar society seldom spoke on the radio, for example.

When two people who have not met before talk, they tend to adopt polite language toward each other and speak with equal levels of politeness. Thus changes in lifestyle have induced people to talk more politely.

**women's advances in society**   The fact that women have

79

come to play a more important role in society has had an extremely large impact on polite language. Women traditionally talk more politely than men; and traditionally, men have tended to talk more politely in the presence of women. Thus, in situations where women work with men, men have gradually come to employ more polite language.

People often say that women have come to speak like men, but at the same time, men have come to talk like women. For instance, men used to use such words as "*cha*" (tea), "*kashi*" (sweets), and "*bentoo*" (box lunch) without "*o*," but nowadays it is common for men to add the "*o*" to these words. Another example is the various pronouns like "*jibun*" (I), "*washi*" (I) and "*kisama*" (you) used by men in prewar Japan. These were regarded as exclusively men's terms, but these words are seldom used now. Even in verbs we can see women's influence on men's speech; men use "*taberu*" (eat) more often than "*kuu*" (eat; masculine, familiar) now.

**refined speech**    To summarize the present tendency in the use of polite language, people have come, and will continue, to use a language that is polite-sounding and less discriminatory. This might be called "refined speech" rather than "polite speech" because it reflects the speaker's concern for a pleasant tone rather than concern with relative social rank.

In the following discussion of expressions of respect, humbleness and reserve, we will refer to such changes whenever necessary, while trying to clarify the traditional rules of politeness.

## 2.   The Expression of Respect

**expressions of respect**    Respectful expressions are used when one politely refers to others or describes their condition or actions. The expressions of respect can be divided into the following four groups:

1. expressions showing respect toward a person
2. expressions showing respect toward a person's belongings (including members of their family)
3. expressions showing respect toward a person's condition
4. expressions showing respect toward a person's actions

The use of expressions of respect is limited to cases where the speaker has personal relations with that person or personal feelings toward him or her. Namely, one does not use expressions of respect when referring to persons in history.

> *Oda Nobunaga-wa yonjuu-hassai-de shinda.* (Oda Nobunaga [1534-82] died at the age of 48.)

In the same way one usually does not use expressions of respect when referring to contemporaries like well-known writers, actors or actresses, scholars and statesmen unless one has special feelings of respect toward them.

> *Kakefu-wa kono-goro yoku utte-ru-ne.* (Kakefu — a baseball player — is hitting well these days.)

> *Hasegawa Kazuo-wa ii haiyuu-deshita.* (Hasegawa Kazuo was a good actor.)

## (1) Respect toward a person

**terms of respect**     One shows respect toward others by using various terms of respect. Terms of respect are added to (1) personal names, (2) family terms, (3) professions, (4) positions, and (5) situations. Of the terms of respect, "*san*" is the most commonly used; "*sama*" is more polite than "*san*," and "*chan*" sounds more familiar than "*san*." Besides these three, "position names" such as "*sensee*" (professor, teacher) and "*shachoo*" (company director) are also used as terms of respect.

81

It is important to remember that terms of respect are never used with one's own name in Japanese. In English it is common to say things like "This is **Mr.** Jones speaking," or "I'm **Mrs.** Smith." But it is strange to say things like *"*Kochira-wa Joonzu-**san**-desu," or *"*Watashi-wa Sumisu-**san**-desu" in Japanese.

a) personal names plus terms of respect

When one politely addresses or refers to someone, it is most common to use a personal name plus a term of respect, as in

Tanaka-**san** (Mr./Mrs./Miss/Ms. Tanaka)

Kazuo-**san** (Kazuo; a man's name)

Yoshiko-**san** (Yoshiko; a woman's name)

It should be noted that "*san*" is added to both family names and first names, and both men's names and women's names. The same applies to "*sama*"; "*chan*," being familiar, is usually added to first names only.

Tanaka-**san**, okusan-kara denwa-desu-yo. (Mr. Tanaka, there's a telephone call from your wife — said by a colleague)

Tanaka-**sama**, Suzuki-**sama**-ga shoomen-genkan-de omachi-de-gozaimasu. (Mrs. Tanaka, Mrs. Suzuki is waiting for you at the main entrance — paging a customer in a department store)

Yoshiko-**chan**-wa gakkoo-kara kaerimashita-ka. (Is Yoshiko back from school yet? — a neighbor asking Yoshiko's mother)

When addressing someone, it is most common to add a term of respect to the name. Addressing someone or referring to someone by just a name, either first or last, is quite limited in Japanese. Young people sometimes use the first names of their friends without terms of respect, close male friends sometimes address

82

each other by their last names, and sometimes older members of a group or superiors at work will address younger persons in this way. Otherwise, usually a term of respect is added when addressing someone. At home, parents sometimes add *"san"* or *"chan"* to the first names of their children; this is more often done by mothers.

Addressing someone by their name alone should be avoided unless you are asked to do so. When speaking in English, it is all right to call someone "Kazuo" or "Yoshiko," but this should be done with care when speaking in Japanese. Even if your young Japanese friends have asked you to call them by their names without *"san,"* it is advisable to add *"san"* when speaking or referring to them in the presence of their parents.

b) family terms

When directly addressing or talking about older members of one's family, usually the polite prefix *"o"* and *"san/sama/chan"* are used as in

**Otoosan,** *itte-rasshai.* (Bye, Father — said when Father leaves home.)

**Okaasan,** *doko-e iku-no.* (Where are you going, Mother?)

**Oniisan***-wa doko-ni iru?* (Where is Big Brother now? —said by a younger brother or sister. His first name is used in English in this situation.)

**Oneesan***-mo taberu?* (Are you going to eat it, too, Big Sister? — said by a younger brother or sister. Her first name is used in English.)

When addressing or referring to a younger member of the family, one uses the first name with or without *"san/chan."*

MOTHER: **Yoshiko-chan,** *gohan-da-kara, minna-o yonde.* (Yoshiko, dinner is ready. Call everybody, will you?)
YOSHIKO: *Hai. . . .Ano-ne,* **Okaasan, Otoosan***-ga gofun*

83

*matte-tte.* (Yes. . . . Mom, Dad wants to have it five minutes later.)

And the mother usually uses *"Otoosan"* as in

MOTHER: *Soo. Jaa,* **Otoosan**-*o machimashoo.* (All right. Let's wait for Dad.)

Family terms are usually decided from the viewpoint of the youngest person; thus the mother most commonly calls her husband *"Otoosan"* and her older son *"Oniisan,"* just as her youngest child would.

**family terms used for "I"**    Within the family, older persons often refer to themselves just as the children do, instead of using the words *"watashi"* or *"boku."* Namely, the mother will use *"Okaasan"* to refer to herself as in

MOTHER: **Okaasan**-*wa kyoo chotto dekakeru-wa.* (I am going to go out for a while today.)

And an older boy will say something like

OLDER BROTHER: **Niisan**-*ga yatte-yaru-yo.* (I'll do it for you.)

This custom remains even after the children are grown. When the son gets married and has his own children and starts calling himself *"Otoosan,"* his father now will call himself *"Ojiisan"* (Grandfather), seeing himself from the viewpoint of his grandchild, the youngest member of the family. This custom is observed even when grandparents do not live with their son's family.

**using one's spouse's family terms**    Both a husband and wife refer to their spouse's family with the same terms used by the spouse. Suppose the son of a family gets married; his wife will call her husband's mother *"Okaasan"* just as she does with her own mother, and he will call his wife's parents *"Otoosan"* and *"Okaasan."*

84

When they need to distinguish their own parents from the parents of their spouse, they will use some device like adding the name of the place where the parents live, as in "*Nakano-no Okaasan.*" Or, a man might refer to his own mother as "*Ofukuro*" and to his wife's mother as "*Okaasan.*" And one often refers to one's spouse's family more politely.

A wife may say to her husband:

WIFE: *Kyoo, Nakano-no Okaasan-ga* **irasshatta**-*wa.* (Mother in Nakano came to see us today.)
HUSBAND: *Soo. Genki-datta?* (Did she? How was she?)
WIFE: **Ogenki**-*datta-wa.* (She was fine.)

In this case we can tell that the husband's mother came because the wife used respectful expressions like "*irasshatta*" in place of "*kita*" (came) and "*ogenki*" in place of "*genki*" (fine). If she were talking about her own mother's visit, she would not use such expressions. A husband will also use respectful expressions when referring to his wife's parents, although men generally do not speak as politely as women do.

HUSBAND: *Kyoo, Nakano-no Okaasan-ga* **mieta**-*yo.* (Mother in Nakano came to see us today — "*mieta*" is more polite than "*kita.*")
WIFE: *Soo. Genki-datta?* (*lit.* Was she fine?)
HUSBAND: *Un.* (Yes.)

c) professions

Most names of professions are used, with the addition of "*san*," to address or refer to the person engaged in them.

i) storekeepers

| | |
|---|---|
| greengrocery keeper | *Yaoya-**san*** |
| fishmonger | *Sakanaya-**san*** |
| butcher | *Nikuya-**san*** |
| flower shop keeper | *Hanaya-**san*** |
| bookstore keeper | *Hon'ya-**san*** |

85

| dry cleaner | *Kuriininguya-***san** |
| liquor shop keeper | *Sakaya-***san** |
| electric appliance shop keeper | *Denkiya-***san** |
| photo shop keeper | *Shashin'ya-***san** |

When talking with them in personal situations, one uses the person's name as in "Tanaka-*san*" or "Yamamoto-*san*." And one can also use the name of the shop plus "*san*" as in "Sagamiya-*san*." ("Sagamiya" is often used as a name for liquor stores.)

ii) transportation-related

| drivers of trains, taxis, buses | *Untenshu-***san** |
| conductor | *Shashoo-***san** |
| railway station employees | *Ekiin-***san** |

iii) public service

| policeman | *Omawari-***san** |

iv) others

| doctor | *Oisha-***san** *("Sensee"* in direct address) |
| nurse | *Kangofu-***san** |

The word "*Sensee*" is used as a term of respect as well as to mean "teacher." Namely, it is used to refer to someone else being a teacher, as in

*Nakamura-san-wa shoogakkoo-no* **sensee**-*desu.* (Mrs. Nakamura teaches in an elementary school.)

It is used as a term of respect added to a personal name as in

*Nakamura-***sensee**-*wa ima doko-desu-ka.* (Where is Mrs. Nakamura now?)

"*Sensee*" by itself is also used when referring to a person.

STUDENT A: *Kore, doo suru-no.* (What should I do with this?)

STUDENT B: *Wakaranai. Sensee-ni kiite-mitara?* (I don't

86

know. Why don't you ask the teacher? — The teacher's name is used in English.)

STUDENT'S MOTHER: *Sensee-wa dochira-ni osumai-desu-ka.* (Where do you live?)
TEACHER: *Nakano-ni sunde-imasu.* (I live in Nakano.)

Thus "*Sensee*" is used where an English-speaking person will say "he/she" or "you." When there is no need to distinguish one teacher from another, just "*Sensee*" is used rather than including the last name as in "Nakamura-*sensee.*"

"*Sensee*" is used not only for those engaged in teaching, but also for such professionals as doctors, lawyers, statesmen and leading artists and artisans. Since it implies respect in itself, it is not appropriate to use it in referring to oneself as in *"Watashi-wa shoogakkoo-no sensee-desu*" (I am an elementary school teacher). Instead, one should say "*Shoogakkoo-de oshiete-imasu*" (I teach in an elementary school) or "*Shoogakkoo-no kyooshi-desu*" (I am an elementary school teacher — the word "*kyooshi*" just refers to the profession and does not imply respect).

d) positions

Position names worthy of respect are also used as terms of respect.

i) words ending in "*-choo*" (head)

Words with "*-choo,*" which means "head" or "chief," are used as terms of respect either together with personal names or by themselves.

| | |
|---|---|
| Yamada-*shachoo* | Mr. Yamada, director of the company |
| *Shachoo* | Director of the company |

VISITOR: *Shachoo-ni ome-ni kakaritai-n-desu-ga.* (I'd like to see the director of the company — polite.)
SECRETARY: *Oyakusoku-deshoo-ka.* (Do you have an appointment, sir/ma'am?)

To give several of the most commonly used words with "-*choo*":

| | |
|---|---|
| *Kachoo* | Section chief |
| *Kakarichoo* | Chief clerk |
| *Buchoo* | Division chief |
| *Rijichoo* | Director of the board of trustees |
| *Gakuchoo* | President of a university |
| *Koochoo* | Head of a school |
| *Gichoo* | Chairman |
| *Iinchoo* | Chairman of a committee |

ii) high-ranking statesmen

Such words as "*daijin*" (minister) and "*shushoo*" (prime minister) are also used as terms of respect.

> *Yamada Monbu-**Daijin**-wa kon'ya shuppatsu-shimasu.* (Mr. Yamada, Minister of Education, will leave this evening.)

> ***Shushoo**-wa ima doko-ni irasshaimasu-ka.* (Where is the Prime Minister now?)

iii) academic rank

Such words as "*kyooju*" (professor) and "*hakase*" or "*hakushi*" (doctor, holder of a Ph.D) are also used as terms of respect:

> NEWS REPORTER: *Kono mondai-ni tsuite **Hakase**-no goiken-o ukagaitai-no-desu-ga.* (I'd like to hear your opinion about this, sir.)

iv) other positions

People having high ranks in traditional arts and sports are also referred to by special position names which imply respect:

| | |
|---|---|
| *Shishoo* | Master — used toward leader in classical Japanese music and arts |
| *Sekitori* | High-ranking sumo wrestler |

THE EXPRESSION OF RESPECT

*Yokozuna*    Grand Champion sumo wrestler

e) Situations

When the driver of a taxi wants to attract the attention of a customer who has left something behind, he will call out

> **Okyakusan,** *wasuremono-desu-yo.* (Hey, you forgot something — *lit.* Mr. Customer, there's something left here.)

The word *"kyaku"* means "customer" or "visitor"; here, the polite prefix *"o"* and the term of respect *"san"* are added. *"Okyakusan"* is used in this way by drivers and by storekeepers. In department stores, expensive restaurants, and hotels, where employees use very polite speech, *"Okyakusama"* is used.

*"Okyakusan"* or *"Okyakusama"* are also used to refer to visitors, as in

> MOTHER: **Okyakusama**-*ni goaisatsu-o nasai.* (Say Good afternoon to the visitor — the visitor's name would be used in English.)
> CHILD: *Hai.* (Yes.)

There are still other terms used to refer to a person's situation. *"Otsuresama"* is one of them: *"tsure"* means company.

> RESTAURANT EMPLOYEE: *Nanmee-sama-desu-ka.* (How many will that be? — *"sama"* is added in this way when politely asking how many are in a group.)
> CUSTOMER: *Sannin-desu-kedo, hitori-wa ato-kara kimasu.* (Three, but one will be coming later.)
> . . . after a while . . .
> RESTAURANT EMPLOYEE: **Otsuresama**-*ga omie-ni narimashita.* (Your friend is here — polite.)

**use of pronouns**    Pronouns are not used as often in Japanese as in English; they are left out whenever they can be

89

understood from the context. In addition, one must keep in mind that most of the pronouns do not show respect.

*anata*: "*Anata*" is used toward one's equals or inferiors, not to one's superiors. It is not polite to use "*anata*" when addressing someone you should show respect to. You should use other words such as the person's name plus "*san/sama/sensee*," etc. or a position name like "*sensee*" or "*shachoo*."

*kare, kanojo*: "*Kare*" (he) and "*kanojo*" (she) can be used only when you do not have to show respect to the person. It is impolite to refer to your superior with "*kare*" or "*kanojo*." You should use other polite terms or "*ano-kata*" (more polite than "*ano-hito*").

*-tachi* and *-gata*: The suffix "*-tachi*" means ". . . and others." "*Takahashi-san-tachi*" usually means *Takahashi-san* and other members of his/her group. To refer to Mr. and Mrs. Takahashi, one says "*Takahashi-san-to okusan*" or "*Takahashi-san-fuufu*" in neutral speech. To be respectful, one says "*Takahashi-gofusai*." When using names of professions or positions, "*-gata*" is used as a respectful plural suffix, as in

*Sensee-**gata**-ga irasshaimashita.* (The professors came.)

Thus, to indicate the plural for people, "*-tachi*" is added in neutral speech, and "*-gata*" in respectful speech.

## (2) Respect toward a person's belongings

**someone else's belongings** When referring to someone else's belongings, it is polite to add the honorific prefix "*o*" or "*go*." Since these prefixes serve to indicate whom one is talking about, words meaning "your" or "his/her/their" are usually left out.

***Otaku**-wa dochira-desu-ka.* (Where is your house located?)

***Onamae**-o koko-ni kaite-kudasai.* (Please write your name here.)

90

*Goshokugyoo-mo okaki-kudasai.* (Would you please write down your occupation, too?)

While most words are used with "*o*," kanji compounds are generally used with "*go*."

| | |
|---|---|
| *o-taku* | your/his/her/their house |
| *o-sumai* | your/his/her/their house |
| *o-yoofuku* | your/his/her/their clothes |
| *o-shigoto* | your/his/her/their work |
| *o-kosan* | your/his/her/their child/children |
| *go-kyoodai* | your/his/her/their brothers and sisters |
| *go-kazoku* | your/his/her/their family |
| *go-ryooshin* | your/his/her/their parents |
| *go-kenkyuu* | your/his/her/their study |
| *go-byooki* | your/his/her/their illness |

VISITOR: *Ii osumai-desu-ne.* (You have a very nice house — more literally, It is a very nice house of yours.)
HOST: *Iie.* (No, no.)

ACQUAINTANCE A: *Goryooshin-wa ogenki-desu-ka.* (How are your parents?)
ACQUAINTANCE B: *Hai, okagesama-de.* (Fine, thank you.)

**someone else's family**    To refer to someone else's relatives politely, the following terms are used:

| | | | |
|---|---|---|---|
| *otoosan\** | *otoosama\** | (your/his/her/their) | father |
| *okaasan\** | *okaasama\** | (your/his/her/their) | mother |
| *oniisan\** | *oniisama\** | (your/his/her/their) | older brother |
| *oneesan\** | *oneesama\** | (your/his/her/their) | older sister |
| *otootosan* | *otootosama* | (your/his/her/their) | younger brother |
| *imootosan* | *imootosama* | (your/his/her/their) | younger sister |
| *gokyoodai* | | (your/his/her/their) | brothers and sisters |
| *musukosan, botchan* | *obotchama* | (your/his/her/their) | son |

(Continued on next page)

91

(Continued from previous page)

| | | | |
|---|---|---|---|
| musumesan, ojoosan | ojoosama | (your/his/her/their) | daughter |
| ojisan* | ojisama*, ojigosama | (your/his/her/their) | uncle |
| obasan* | obasama*, obagosama | (your/his/her/their) | aunt |
| ojiisan* | ojiisama* | (your/his/her/their) | grandfather |
| obaasan* | obaasama* | (your/his/her/their) | grandmother |
| omagosan | omagosama | (your/his/her/their) | grandchildren |
| oigosan | oigosama | (your/his/her/their) | nephew |
| meegosan | meegosama | (your/his/her/their) | niece |

Terms ending with "*sama*" are very polite and used more often in letters than in conversation. Women sometimes use them when speaking very politely.

The terms marked with asterisks are also used when directly addressing members of one's own family, as in

**Otoosan,** *hayaku kaette-ne.* (Come home early, Father.)

**Obaasama,** *arigatoo-gozaimashita.* (Thank you very much, Grandma.)

## (3) Respect toward a person's condition

**"o" added to words describing someone's condition**

"*O*" or "*go*" is added to adjectives and adverbs when describing someone's condition politely.

*O*hayai-desu-ne. (You're early — said when meeting someone early in the morning or when someone has arrived early.)

*Takahashi-sensee-wa mada owakai-desu.* (Professor Takahashi is still young.)

*Ano-kata-wa itsumo goyukkuri-desu.* (He always comes rather late.)

*Sensee-wa ogenki-de-irasshaimasu-ne.* (You look very well, Professor.)

92

**"o" added to adjectives**  Not all adjectives are used with "o" or "go." Adjectives having good implications are apt to be used in this way, while those with poor implications are not.

| Adjectives often used with "o" or "go" | | | Adjectives seldom used with "o" or "go" | |
|---|---|---|---|---|
| o- | hayai | (early) | osoi | (late) |
| o- | joozu | (skillful) | heta | (unskillful) |
| o- | kiree | (pretty) | | |
| go- | shinsetsu | (kind) | fushinsetsu | (unkind) |
| go- | nesshin | (enthusiastic) | funesshin | (not enthusiastic) |

Some adjectives are not used "o" or "go" but with the "te(de)-irassharu" form instead.

Takahashi-sensee-wa honto-ni kinben-**de irasshai-masu**. (Prof. Takahashi works really hard.)

**"te(de)-irassharu" for "te(de)-iru"**  To express respect toward someone's condition, the "te(de)-irassharu" pattern is used either with "o" plus an adjective or with a verb.

a) with "o" and adjective

Ohayaku**te-irasshaimasu**-ne. (You're early — more polite than "Ohayai-desu-ne.")

Takahashi-sensee-wa mada owakaku**te-irasshaimasu**. (Prof. Takahashi is still young — more polite than "Takahashi-sensee-wa mada owakai-desu.")

Sensee-wa ogenki-**de-irasshaimasu**-ne. (You look very well, Professor — more polite than "Sensee-wa ogenki-desu-ne.")

(With -i adjectives, "te-irasshaimasu" is used, while with -na adjectives, "de-irasshaimasu" is used.)

b) with verbs (without "o")

When a verb plus "te-iru" is used to describe someone's condi-

93

tion (rather than his/her actions), "*te-irassharu*" is used as the polite form.

| | | |
|---|---|---|
| *yasete-iru* | (to be thin) | — *yasete-irassharu* |
| *futotte-iru* | (to be stout) | — *futotte-irassharu* |
| *nite-iru* | (to be alike, resemble) | — *nite-irassharu* |
| *kekkon-shite-iru* | (to be married) | — *kekkon-shite-irassharu* |

*Ano gokyoodai-wa yoku ni**te-irasshaimasu**-ne.* (The brothers/sisters look a lot alike.)

## (4) Respect toward a person's actions

There are two ways to respectfully refer to a person's actions: one is to use special verbs and the other is to use special verb patterns.

**special verbs**  There are several special verbs used to show respect toward someone's actions:

| | Neutral | Respectful |
|---|---|---|
| to do | *suru* | *nasaru* |
| to be | *iru* | *irassharu, oide-ni naru* |
| to come | *kuru* | *irassharu, oide-ni naru* |
| to go | *iku* | *irassharu, oide-ni naru* |
| to say | *yuu* | *ossharu* |
| to see | *miru* | *goran-ni naru* |
| to eat | *taberu* | *meshiagaru* |
| to drink | *nomu* | *meshiagaru* |
| to wear | *kiru* | *omeshi-ni naru* |
| to die | *shinu* | *nakunaru, onakunari-ni naru* |
| to know | *shitte-iru* | *gozonji* (used with *-desu*) |

ACQUAINTANCE A: *Sensee-wa ima dochira-ni **irasshaimasu**-ka.* (Where is the professor now?)
ACQUAINTANCE B: *Daigaku-ni **oide-ni naru**-to omoimasu.* (I think he is at the university.)

94

THE EXPRESSION OF RESPECT

ACQUAINTANCE A: *Oishasan-wa nante* **osshaimashita?** (What did the doctor say?)

ACQUAINTANCE B: *Taishita koto-wa nai-to* **osshaimashita.** (He said it is not serious.)

HOST: *Doozo hitotsu* **meshiagatte-**kudasai. (Please have some.)

**special verb patterns** There are several verb patterns used to politely refer to someone's action, namely (1) "*o*" plus stem plus "*ni naru*," (2) "*o*" plus stem plus "*desu*," and (3) -(*a*)*reru*.

a) "*o*" plus stem plus "*ni naru*"*

"*O*" plus stem followed by "*ni naru*" is used with almost any verb except those usually replaced by special verbs such as the ones listed above.

|  | Neutral | Respectful |
|---|---|---|
| to read | *yomu* | *oyomi-ni naru* |
| to write | *kaku* | *okaki-ni naru* |
| to walk | *aruku* | *oaruki-ni naru* |
| to stay overnight | *tomaru* | *otomari-ni naru* |
| to buy | *kau* | *okai-ni naru* |
| to sell | *uru* | *ouri-ni naru* |
| to go home | *kaeru* | *okaeri-ni naru* |
| to go out | *(uchi-o) deru* | *ode-ni naru* |

SECRETARY: *Dochira-o saki-ni* **oyomi-ni narimasu**-ka. (Which one are you going to read first?)

DIRECTOR: *Aa, kore-o saki-ni yomoo.* (I'll read this one first.)

ACQUAINTANCE A: *Taitee asa nanji-goro* **ode-ni narimasu**-ka. (What time do you usually leave in the morning?)

---

* Sometimes "*nasaru*" is used instead of "*ni naru*" as in "*oyomi-nasaru*" (ex. *Oyomi-nasaimashita* — He read it), but this sounds old-fashioned and is used chiefly by older persons.

95

ACQUAINTANCE B: *Kuji-goro demasu.* (I leave around nine.)

Incidentally, *"o"* plus stem plus *"kudasai"* is used as a polite and refined expression when making a request. In this case *"ni natte"* has been left out.

|  | Polite | More polite |
|---|---|---|
| enter | *haitte-kudasai* | *ohairi-kudasai* |
| read | *yonde-kudasai* | *oyomi-kudasai* |
| write | *kaite-kudasai* | *okaki-kudasai* |
| sit down | *kakete-kudasai* | *okake-kudasai* |

b) *"o"* plus stem plus *"desu"*

This form is often used in place of *"o"* plus stem plus *"ni naru"*; this sounds more indirect and reserved. Namely, saying

*Nanji-goro* **okaeri-desu-***ka.* (What time are you going home?)

sounds more reserved than saying

*Nanji-goro* **okaeri-ni narimasu-***ka.*

Thus, the following expressions are used very often:

A NEIGHBOR: *Ohayoo-gozaimasu. Kore-kara* **odekake-desu-***ka.* (Good morning. Have a nice day — *lit.* Are you going out now?)

ACQUAINTANCE A: *Konban-wa dochira-ni* **otomari-desu-***ka.* (Where are you staying tonight?)
ACQUAINTANCE B: *X Hoteru-ni tomarimasu.* (I'll stay at X Hotel.)

STRANGER A (pointing to a public phone): *Kono denwa,* **otsukai-desu-***ka.* (Are you using this phone?)
STRANGER B: *Iie, moo sumimashita. Doozo.* (No, I'm through. Please go ahead.)

c) *-(a)reru*

This form is made by adding "*-reru*" to the negative base of *-u* verbs like "*iku*," and "*-rareru*" to that of *-ru* verbs like "*miru*."

> *iku* → *ikareru* (*-u* verb)
>
> *miru* → *mirareru* (*-ru* verb)
>
> *suru* → *sareru* (irregular verb)
>
> *kuru* → *korareru* (irregular verb)

Actually this form is the same as the form used for the passive voice.

This way of expressing respect is rather formal and reserved-sounding; it is most often used in official announcements or public speech:

> *Shushoo-wa konban Chuugoku-yori kikoku-***saremashita***.* (The Prime Minister returned from China this evening — announcement made by an official.)

> *Daijin-wa kore-ni tsuite doo* ***kangaeraremasu****-ka.* (What do you think about this, Mr. Minister? — asked by a newspaper reporter.)

In daily conversation men use this more often than women; women more frequently use "*o . . . ni naru*."

The recent tendency is to use "*-(a)reru*" when talking with strangers. People tend to use this form more often when speaking to a stranger than when speaking with their acquaintances because it still sounds rather formal. The fact that men use it more often than women can be attributed to the fact that men usually have more chances to talk with strangers than women do.

## 3. The Expression of Humility

Humble expressions are used to refer to oneself, persons or things associated with oneself, one's condition, and one's actions

97

when speaking politely. In the first three cases only a small number of humble terms are used, while in the last, namely when referring to one's own actions, various humble expressions are used.

## (1) The expression of humility about oneself, one's associates and one's condition

**humble expressions meaning "we," "us"** In letter-writing and formal speech special expressions are used to refer to oneself or one's associates. In very old-fashioned speech too, some people use such words as *"gusai"* (my wife — *lit.* my foolish wife) or *"gusoku"* (my son —*lit.* my foolish son), but in ordinary conversation only a few words are used to specifically refer to oneself or to persons or things associated with oneself.

To refer to oneself, *"watashi"* is used in any situation, but when humbly referring to one's group members including oneself, *"watashi-domo"* is used instead of *"watashi-tachi."* When referring to people with respect, *"-gata"* is used instead of *"-tachi."* (cf. p.90)

SHOPKEEPER: *Ainiku sono shina-wa* **watashidomo**-*dewa atsukatte-orimasen.* (I'm sorry we do not handle that article.)

HOUSEWIFE: **Watashidomo**-*wa sono hi-wa rusu-ni itashimasu-node yoroshiku onegai-itashimasu.* (We are going to be away on that day. I'm sorry we can't join you — said to a neighbor who has asked them to participate in some community activity.)

**humble expressions about one's associates** On very formal occasions special terms are used to refer to the company where one works such as *"heesha"* (our company — *lit.* poor company) in contrast with *"kisha"* (your company — *lit.* precious company). But in daily conversation humble expressions about one's associates for the most part concern family terms.

## THE EXPRESSION OF HUMILITY

When referring to one's own family in conversation with someone outside the family, one should try not to add "*san*" or "*chan*" as in "*Uchi-no Yoshiko-chan-ga . . .*" (Our Yoshiko . . .) or "*uchi-no akachan*" (our baby). Instead one should use such terms as "*kodomo*" or "*akanboo.*" The following is a list of the family terms used to refer to them humbly.

| | | |
|---|---|---|
| my/our | father | *chichi* |
| my/our | mother | *haha* |
| my/our | elder brother | *ani* |
| my/our | elder sister | *ane* |
| my/our | younger brother | *otooto* |
| my/our | younger sister | *imooto* |
| my/our | brothers & sisters | *kyoodai* |
| my/our | grandfather | *sofu* |
| my/our | grandmother | *sobo* |
| my/our | child | *kodomo* |
| my/our | son | *musuko* |
| my/our | daughter | *musume* |
| my | husband | *shujin* |
| my | wife | *kanai* |

**humble expressions about one's condition**    One uses respectful adjectives like "*ohayai*" and "*owakai*" when referring to other persons, but there is not much difference between descriptions of one's own condition in humble speech and non-humble speech. One difference comes when using the "*te-iru*" pattern to describe condition as in

*yasete-iru* (to be thin)
*kekkon-shite-iru* (to be married)

*oru*:    One can use "*te-oru*" instead to show humility. Namely, to mean "I live in Tokyo," one says in non-humble speech

*Tookyoo-ni sunde-imasu.* (polite)

99

*Tookyoo-ni sunde-ru.* (familiar)

and in humble speech

*Tookyoo-ni* **sunde-orimasu.**

*gozaimasu:* Another humble expression is *"de-gozaimasu"* as in

*Hai, Yamamoto-**de-gozaimasu.*** (This is the Yamamoto residence — said largely by women when answering the telephone.)

To be humble, one adds *"de-gozaimasu"* to one's name when introducing oneself:

*Hajimemashite. Yamamoto-**de-gozaimasu.*** (How do you do? My name is Yamamoto.)

It is impolite to use *"de-gozaimasu"* with the second or third person as in

*\*Shitsuree-desu-ga, Katoo-sensee-de-gozaimasu-ka.* (Excuse me. Are you Prof. Kato?)

Instead one should say

*Shitsuree-desu-ga, Katoo-sensee-**de-irasshaimasu**-ka.*

to mean the same thing.

Saying *"Shitsuree-de-gozaimasu-ga"* instead of *"Shitsuree-desu-ga"* is humble speech.

In addition,

*Mooshiwake **gozaimasen.*** (I am very sorry.)

is used as a more humble version of

*Mooshiwake arimasen.*

## (2) The expression of humility about one's actions

There are two types of humble expressions used when talking about one's own actions; one are expressions concerning actions which are independent of other persons, and the second are those concerning actions which are related in some way with others.

**humble expressions about actions independent of others** In polite speech one sometimes uses humble expressions even when talking about one's own actions which are unrelated with other persons. Two verbs are used for this purpose: *"oru"* and *"itasu."* These humble verbs are also used for actions performed by others in one's family.

a) *oru*

The verb *"oru"* (to be) is used in place of *"iru"* as in

ACQUAINTANCE A: *Nichiyoobi-wa taitee odekake-desu-ka.* (Do you usually go out on Sunday?)
ACQUAINTANCE B: *Iie, taitee uchi-ni* **orimasu.** (No, I usually stay home.)

ACQUAINTANCE *Otoosama-wa ima dochira-ni irasshai-masu-ka.* (Where is your father now?)
HOUSEWIFE: *Ima niwa-ni* **orimasu.** *Yonde-mairimashoo-ka.* (He is in the garden now. Shall I call him?)

b) *itasu*

The verb *"itasu"* (to do) is often used in place of *"suru."*

ACQUAINTANCE A: *Oshigoto-wa?* (What's your occupation?)
ACQUAINTANCE B: *Shuppan-o* **itashite**-*orimasu.* (I work in publishing.)

ACQUAINTANCE A: *Goshujin-wa donna oshigoto-desu-ka.* (What does your husband do?)
ACQUAINTANCE B: *Bengoshi-o* **itashite**-*orimasu.* (He's a lawyer — *lit.* He is doing a lawyer.)

101

c) other verbs

There are several other humble verbs commonly used in the same way:

| | Non-humble | Humble |
|---|---|---|
| to eat | *taberu* | *itadaku* |
| to come | *kuru* | *mairu* |
| to go | *iku* | *mairu* |
| to say | *yuu* | *moosu* |

HOUSEWIFE A: *Otaku-dewa asa donna mono-o meshiagarimasu-ka.* (What do you have for breakfast? — respectful)

HOUSEWIFE B: *Uchi-dewa gohan-to omisoshiru-o* **itadakimasu.** (We have cooked rice and *miso* soup — humble)

HOUSEWIFE A: *Goshujin-wa kyoo-wa nanji-goro okaeri-desu-ka.* (What time is your husband coming home today?)

HOUSEWIFE B: *Saa, nanimo* **mooshimasen**-*deshita-kara, rokuji-goro kaette-***mairimasu**-*deshoo.* (Well, he didn't say anything about it; he should be back around six.)

**humble expressions about actions related to others** As in the case of expressions of respect, humble expressions about one's actions related to others are of two types, special verbs and special verb patterns.

a) special verbs

Several different words are used as humble expressions to refer to visiting someone. To mean "I will come to see you" various humble expressions such as *"mairu," "ukagau,"* and *"ojama-suru"* are used:

*Ashita sanji-ni ukagaimasu.* (I will come to see you tomorrow at 3.)

*Ashita sanji-ni ojama-shimasu.*

102

*Ashita sanji-ni mairimasu.*

All three are commonly used, although probably the first two are used more frequently than the last one.

The following is a list of special verbs commonly used to humbly refer to one's actions that are related in some way with other persons:

| | Non-humble | Humble |
|---|---|---|
| to go visit someone | *iku* | *ukagau, ojama-suru, mairu* |
| to do | *suru* | *itasu* |
| to tell | *yuu, hanasu* | *mooshiageru* |
| to see something | *miru* | *haiken-suru* |
| to see someone | *au* | *ome-ni kakaru* |
| to hear | *kiku* | *ukagau* |
| to borrow | *kariru* | *haishaku-suru* |
| to give | *ageru* | *sashiageru* |
| to be given, receive | *morau* | *itadaku* |
| to know something | *shitte-iru* | *zonjite-oru* |
| to think | *omou* | *zonjiru* |
| to know someone | *shitte-iru* | *zonjiagete-oru* |

VISITOR TO A COMPANY: *Shachoo-ni **ome-ni kakaritai**-n-desu-ga.* (I'd like to see the director.)
SECRETARY: *Oyakusoku-deshoo-ka.* (Do you have an appointment, sir/ma'am?)

ACQUAINTANCE A: *Kobayashi-san-ga oyame-ni natta koto, gozonji-deshita-ka.* (Did you know that Mr. Kobayashi quit?)
ACQUAINTANCE B: *Iie, **zonjimasen**-deshita. Ima hajimete **ukagaimashita**.* (No, I didn't know that. This is the first I've heard of it.)

ACQUAINTANCE A: *Yamamoto-san-o gozonji-desu-ka.* (Do you know Mr. Yamamoto?)
ACQUAINTANCE B: *Hai, **zonjiagete-orimasu**.* (Yes, I know him.)

103

b) special verb patterns
  i) "o" plus stem plus "suru"
  To refer to one's actions in relationship with others, "o" plus "suru" is used with ordinary verbs; the following is a list of some common words often used in this form:

|  | Non-humble | Humble |
|---|---|---|
| I'll carry it for you. | Mochimasu. | Omochi-shimasu. |
| I'll wait for you. | Machimasu. | Omachi-shimasu. |
| I'll deliver it to you. | Todokemasu. | Otodoke-shimasu. |
| I'll pay you. | Haraimasu. | Oharai-shimasu. |
| I'll inform you. | Shirasemasu. | Oshirase-shimasu. |
| I'll send it to you. | Okurimasu. | Ookuri-shimasu. |
| I'll return it to you. | Kaeshimasu. | Okaeshi-shimasu. |
| I'll teach you. | Oshiemasu. | Ooshie-shimasu. |
| I'll telephone you. | Denwa-shimasu. | Odenwa-shimasu. |

ACQUAINTANCE A: **Omachi-shite**-orimasu-kara, zehi oide-kudasai. (We'll be waiting for you. Please by all means come.)
ACQUAINTANCE B: Arigatoo-gozaimasu. Zehi ukagaimasu. (Thank you. I will by all means come.)

Sometimes "itasu" or "mooshiageru" is used in place of "suru" to make the expression even more humble.

DEPARTMENT STORE EMPLOYEE: Otaku-made **otodoke-itashimashoo**-ka. (Would you like us to deliver it to your house?)
CUSTOMER: Hai, onegai-shimasu. (Yes, thank you.)

TELEPHONE CALLER: Moshimoshi, Yamamoto-sensee-de-irasshaimasu-ka. (Hello, is this Prof. Yamamoto?)
YAMAMOTO: Hai, soo-desu-ga. (Yes, it is.)
TELEPHONE CALLER: Hajimete **odenwa-mooshiagemasu**. Jitsu-wa . . . (Actually you don't know me but . . . lit. I am calling you for the first time. Actually . . .)

THE EXPRESSION OF HUMILITY

"*Onegai-shimasu*" is used as a set expression, but it was originally constructed using this pattern; that is, "*o*" plus "*negai*" plus "*suru*."

Some of the special humble verbs are also used in this "*o*" plus stem plus "*suru*" pattern; "*ukagau*" is one of them:

*o-ukagai-suru* (to visit someone, to ask something)

However the verbs "*mairu*," "*agaru*," "*itasu*," "*mooshiageru*," and "*itadaku*" and the expressions "*haiken-suru*" and "*ome-ni kakaru*" are not used in the "*o*" plus stem plus "*suru*" pattern.

ii) . . . *(a)sete-itadaku*

When excusing oneself from the presence of someone, one uses the humble expression "*Shitsuree-shimasu*" (Please excuse me — *lit.* I'm going to be rude). And to make this more humble "*Shitsuree-suru*" is often combined with "*(a)sete-itadaku*" — the causative form plus "*te-itadaku*" — as in

*Kyoo-wa kore-de shitsuree-**sasete-itadakimasu**.* (I'm going to leave now.)

This literally means "I will receive from you the favor of letting me be rude." This form sounds humble because it implies that one is going to do something with the permission of the listener.

*Ashita-wa **yasumasete-itadakimasu**.* (I would like to be absent tomorrow — said by an employee to his/her boss.)

*Hayame-ni **kaerasete-itadakitai**-n-desu-ga.* (I'd like to be excused a little early today — said by an employee to his/her boss.)

ACQUAINTANCE A: *Kore, kondo deta zasshi-desu.* (This is a new magazine — *i.e.* the first issue.)
ACQUAINTANCE B: *Soo-desu-ka. Chotto **yomasete-itadakemasu**-ka.* (Is that so? May I take a look at it?)

As seen in these examples, this pattern is often used when making

105

requests; *"(a)sete-kudasai"* and *"(a)sete-kudasaimasen-ka"* are also used in requests.

> *Chotto* **yomasete-kudasaimasen**-*ka.* (May I take a look at it?)

## 4. The Expression of Reserve

**politeness and reserve** To be truly polite, one must pay attention not only to levels of speech and showing respect and humbleness but also to showing reserve. Even if one speaks in polite language, using appropriate expressions showing respect toward others and humility about oneself, one can still be impolite. For instance, if someone said to an acquaintance something like

> *\*Ashita otaku-ni oukagai-suru oyakusoku-deshita-ga, tsugoo-ga waruku narimashita-node, yamesasete-itadaki-masu.* (I promised to visit you tomorrow, but it has become inconvenient for me, so I will not be coming.)

it would sound impolite even though the wording is correct. This person used proper humble expressions like *"oukagai-suru"* and *"yamesasete-itadakimasu,"* but failed to show regret over causing the listener inconvenience and hesitancy in talking about the change. In fact, the expression of reserve in large part concerns the indication of such regret or hesitancy.

Expressing reserve is necessary in the following cases:

1. when addressing someone
2. when making a request
3. when expressing one's judgment or opinion
4. when stating one's own wishes or convenience

And the expression of reserve is necessary not only in polite speech but also in familiar speech.

106

## THE EXPRESSION OF RESERVE

**(1) Reserved expressions used when addressing someone**
When addressing someone, either an acquaintance or a stranger, one should indicate reserve through the use of several different expressions.

a) *anoo* (well. . .; excuse me; say. . .)
"*Anoo*" is used when addressing someone, when stating one's opinion, and when making a request:

> PASSERBY A: ***Anoo*** . . . (Excuse me.)
> PASSERBY B: *Hai.* (Yes?)
> PASSERBY A: *Sumimasen-ga kono hen-ni kooban-wa arimasen-ka.* (Sorry to trouble you. Is there a police box near here?)

> SECTION MEMBER: ***Anoo,*** *kachoo* . . . (Excuse me.)
> SECTION CHIEF: *Uun.* . . (Yes . . .)
> SECTION MEMBER: *Oshigoto-chuu, sumimasen-ga.* (Sorry to trouble you while you are working.)

"*Anoo*" is often used as a stopgap phrase when looking for the proper words, but it is also used to indicate hesitancy about troubling someone. In polite speech, "*anoo*" should be pronounced slowly to show hesitancy.

It sounds rude to say "*Chotto!*" to attract the attention of others, even when they are employees in stores or restaurants. It is better to use "*Anoo*" or "*Sumimasen.*"

b) *sumimasen* (excuse me, sorry)
"*Sumimasen,*" often pronounced "*suimasen,*" is used to attract someone's attention with reserve, as well as to express apology. When attracting a waiter's or waitress's attention, "*Sumimasen*" or "*Onegai-shimasu*" is usually used.

> CUSTOMER: ***Sumimasen!*** (Waitress!)
> WAITRESS: *Hai.* (Yes?)
> CUSTOMER: *Biiru, kudasai.* (Give me a beer, please.)

CUSTOMER: *Sumimasen.* (Excuse me.)
POST OFFICE EMPLOYEE: *Hai.* (Yes?)
CUSTOMER: *Kitte kudasai.* (Give me some stamps, please.)

c) *onegai-shimasu* (excuse me)

"*Onegai-shimasu*" is used to attract attention when you want someone to wait on you. When you find nobody around to help you in a store, you should say "*Onegai-shimasu*" instead of *"*Konnichiwa*" (Good day).

d) *moshimoshi* (hello; say)

"*moshimoshi*" is used to attract someone's attention on the phone, and sometimes in other situations as well.

> PASSERBY A (noticing that Passerby B has dropped something): *Moshimoshi, nanika ochimashita-yo.* (Say, you've dropped something!)
> PASSERBY B: *A, doomo sumimasen.* (Oh, thank you very much.)

"*Anoo*" is also used very commonly in this sort of situation.

## (2) Reserved expressions used when making a request

When making a request, one should express one's regrets about having to trouble the other person by using indirect expressions and proper sentence endings.

### expressing regret at troubling others

a) *sumimasen-ga* (*lit.* I'm sorry but)

While "*Sumimasen!*" is used to attract someone's attention, "*Sumimasen-ga*" is used to indicate one's hesitancy about troubling the other person.

> ACQUAINTANCE A (before leaving his office together with his visitor, Acquaintance B): *Sumimasen-ga, chotto koko-de matte-ite-itadakemasen-ka. Chotto shigoto-o katazu-kete-kimasu-node.* (Could you wait here a short while? I'll just finish up some work.)

108

ACQUAINTANCE B: *Ee, doozo goyukkuri.* (That's all right. Please take your time.)

"*Sumimasen-ga*" is most common in such a situation, but there are several other expressions used for the same purpose:

*Osoreirimasu-ga* ... (I'm very sorry to trouble you — formal)

*Mooshiwake arimasen-ga* ... (I'm very sorry to trouble you — very polite)

b) *oisogashii tokoro-o* (*lit.* when you're so busy)

There are several set expressions used when one expresses reserve about making a request. These expressions are used to indicate that one is going to trouble someone although one knows one shouldn't do so. They often use "... *tokoro-o*" (while you are . . .) as part of them:

*oisogashii tokoro-o* (when you're so busy)

*oyasumi-no tokoro-o* (when you are resting)

*konna jikan-ni* (at such an hour)

*yoru osoku* (so late at night)

*asa hayaku* (so early in the morning)

These expressions are used before those discussed in the previous section, as in

*Oisogashii tokoro-o sumimasen-ga* ...

*Oyasumi-no tokoro-o mooshiwake arimasen-ga* ...

*Konna jikan-ni osoreirimasu-ga* ...

*Yoru osoku mooshiwake arimasen-ga* ...

The other person will politely answer with

*Iie, kamaimasen.* (No, I don't mind at all.)

c) *gomeewaku-towa omoimasu-ga* (*lit.* I know it's a nuisance for you but)

Several expressions are used to indicate the speaker's reserve about making a request although aware of the trouble it may cause. To give the most common ones:

*Gomeewaku-towa omoimasu-ga* ... (I know it is a nuisance for you but)

*Otesuu-o okake-shimasu-ga* ... (I'm causing you much trouble but)

*Makoto-ni mooshiagenikui-n-desu-ga* ... (I really hate to ask this but)

### sentence endings showing reserve about a request

a) *(te)-itadakemasen-ka, (te)-kudasaimasen-ka*

These two endings are those most commonly used in reserved requests. ("*te-kudasai*" does not sound very polite and cannot be used in polite requests). They are similar in degree of politeness; the difference, if any, is that the first sounds a little more reserved.

*Moo sukoshi kuwashiku setsumee-shite-**itadakemasen-ka**.* (Could you please explain it in a little more detail?)

*Kore, chotto goran-**kudasaimasen-ka**.* (Would you please take a look at this?)

Before "*itadakemasen-ka*" or "*te-kudasaimasen-ka*" comes either the "*te*" form of a verb, "*o*" plus stem, or "*go*" plus a *kanji* compound (like "*goran*").

To sound more reserved "*masen-deshoo-ka*" is used, as in

*Kore, chotto goran-**itadakemasen-deshoo-ka**.*

"*(te)-itadakemasu-ka*" and "*(te)-kudasaimasu-ka*" are also used but are not as common.

110

As less polite forms of these patterns, *"te-moraemasen-ka"* and *"te-kuremasen-ka"* are used between equals or toward younger persons.

In familiar speech too, one indicates reserve about troubling others with *"te-moraenai?"* and *"te-kurenai?"* In requests where reserve is not needed, *"te"* and *"te-ne"* are used, as in

Chotto matte(-ne). (Wait a moment, will you?)

## (3) Reserved expressions used when stating an opinion
**expressions used before stating an opinion**

a) *soo-desu-nee* (well)

When giving one's opinion with reserve one starts with *"soo-desu-nee"* even when one feels quite definite about it. This use of *"soo-desu-nee"* is surprisingly frequent. If you watch a television program on which an interviewer asks people for their opinions, you will see that almost all of them start off with this expression.

*"Soo-desu-nee"* literally means "That's so, isn't it?" but when used in this situation, it does not indicate agreement, but shows hesitation and thus reserve. In this usage it should be said with a dangling tone as in

So

o

de su ne . . .e. . .
→

without any rise or fall in intonation rather than saying *"Soo-desu-ne"* in one breath.

When it means "That's right," it is said with a falling tone; the "ne" falls after rising slightly.

So        ne ↘

o desu

When it is used to solicit agreement, meaning "That's right, don't you think?," it is said with a rising tone on the *"ne."*

111

*So* *ne* ↗
*o desu*

On the other hand, if it falls and is dragged out with "*nee*," it indicates disapproval.

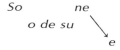

SECTION CHIEF: *Ashita-made-ni dekiru-kana.* (I wonder if this can be done by tomorrow.)
SECTION MEMBER: ***Soo-desu-nee*** ... *Dekireba asatte-ni shite-itadakitai-n-desu-ga.* (Well ... If possible, the day after tomorrow would be better.)

This expression is also used in familiar conversations or by seniors toward juniors, but in the form "*da-nee*" instead of "*desu-nee.*"

SECTION MEMBER: *Kore-de ii-deshoo-ka.* (Is this all right?)
SECTION CHIEF: *Un,* ***soo-da-nee*** ... *Koko-wa chotto naoshita hoo-ga ii-kamo shirenai-ne.* (Well, you might change this part a little bit.)

b) *saa* (well)

This is usually used with such expressions as "*wakarimasen*" (I don't understand) or "*shirimasen*" (I don't know) to show one's reserve about expressing an opinion. At times it is used alone.

ACQUAINTANCE A: *Dotchi-ga ii-deshoo-ne.* (I wonder which is better.)
ACQUAINTANCE B: ***Saa*** ... *yoku wakarimasen-kedo, kotchi-no hoo-ga yosasoo-desu-ne.* (Well, I don't know for sure, but this seems to be better.)

SECTION CHIEF: *Kore-de ii-kana.* (I wonder if this is all right.)

SECTION MEMBER: *Saa* . . . (Well . . .)
SECTION CHIEF: *Hakkiri itte-kure-yo.* (Go ahead and speak frankly.)
SECTION MEMBER: *Hai, jaa* . . . (All right — he starts stating his opinion.)

**adverbs and phrases used to indicate reserve** When giving one's opinion with reserve, several different adverbs and phrases are used to make the tone more indefinite.

a) *doomo* (somehow)

"*Doomo*" means "somehow, very much, indeed." It is used with positive-sounding expressions like "*arigatoo*,"* but it can also imply a negative judgment. The rest of the sentence after "*doomo*" is often left out:

SECTION CHIEF: *Ashita-wa doo?* (How about tomorrow?)
SECTION MEMBER: *Ashita-wa **doomo*** . . . (Tomorrow somehow — a phrase meaning "is not convenient" is implied.)

b) *amari* (not very)

"*Amari*" also implies a negative judgment and can be used with the rest of the sentence omitted.

ACQUAINTANCE A: *Yamamoto-san-ni tanomoo-ka-to omou-n-desu-ga.* (I'm wondering if I should ask Mr. Yamamoto to do it.)
ACQUAINTANCE B: *Ano-hito-wa **amari*** . . . (He is not very . . .)

c) *chotto, sukoshi, shooshoo* (a little)

These words are used to weaken the tone of disapproval or criticism, as in

---

* "*Doomo*" originally precedes expressions of negative form or implication: since "*arigatoo*" originally means "it is difficult to exist," "*doomo*" is appropriate with it. In the same way "*doomo*" is appropriate with "*shitsuree*," which also has a negative meaning.

113

*Koko-wa* **chotto** *kaeta hoo-ga ii-kamo shiremasen.* (It might be best to change this part a little bit.)

Of the three, "*shooshoo*" sounds most formal and "*chotto*" most familiar.

d) *moshika-suru-to* (perhaps)

"*Moshika-suru-to*" and "*moshika-shitara*" are used to indicate that the possibility of something or other is small; the two are quite similar, although the latter sounds slightly more familiar. They are usually followed by "*kamo shiremasen.*"

**Moshika-suru-to** *ame-ga furu-kamo shiremasen-yo.* (It might start raining.)

**reserved sentence endings** When expressing an opinion with reserve, one uses indirect sentence endings rather than definite-sounding ones. For instance, instead of saying

*Yoku arimasen.* (It's not good.)

one will say in reserved speech

*Yoku nai-n-ja nai-deshoo-ka.* (I'm afraid it's not good.)

or

*Yoku nai-n-ja nai-ka-to omoimasu-ga.* (I'm afraid it's not good.)

And one will often use such adverbs as "*amari*" and "*doomo*" as in

*Amari yoku nai-n-ja nai-deshoo-ka.* (I'm afraid it's not very good.)

*Doomo amari yoku nai-n-ja nai-ka-to omoimasu-ga.* (I'm afraid it does not seem to be very good.)

a) *n-ja nai-deshoo-ka.* (I wonder if it is not . . .)/*n-ja nai-ka-to omoimasu-kedo* (I wonder if it is not the case that . . . but)

These sentence endings are used to indicate the speaker's reserve

114

about expressing an opinion and his or her readiness to listen to the other person's opinion. The pattern "*to omoimasu*" is usually followed by "*kedo/keredo/ga*."

> SECTION CHIEF: *Ashita-made-ni dekiru-kane.* (Can it be finished by tomorrow?)
> SECTION MEMBER: *Saa . . . ashita-wa chotto murina-**n-ja nai-ka-to** omoimasu-ga.* (Well, I'm afraid it can't be done by tomorrow.)

When such reserved endings are used in familiar speech, they are used in somewhat different forms:

> SECTION MEMBER: *Kachoo, kore-de yoroshii-deshoo-ka.* (Is this all right, Section Chief?)
> SECTION CHIEF: *Un, soo-da-naa . . . Koko-wa nai hoo-ga ii-**n-ja nai-kana**.* (Well, let me see . . . This part might be left out, don't you think?)

Women usually use "*kashira*" instead of "*kana*":

> *Ee, soo-nee . . . Koko-wa nai hoo-ga ii-**n-ja nai-kashira**.*

b) *kamo shiremasen* (may)

This is used to indicate that the speaker thinks the possibility of something is not very high.

> *Ame-ga furu-**kamo shiremasen**-ne.* (It may start raining.)

> *Moshikasuru-to korarenai-**kamo shiremasen**.* (I'm afraid I may not be able to come.)

c) other sentence endings

To sound reserved, "*deshoo*" is preferred over "*desu*":

> *Kochira-no hoo-ga yoroshii-**deshoo**-ne.* (This might be better.)

Also "*yoo*" (look like) is added to make a sentence sound less definite:

*Kochira-no hoo-ga yoroshii* **yoo**-*ni omoimasu-ga.* (I should think this is better.)

To avoid sounding definite about one's beliefs, *"to omoimasu"* is often replaced by such expressions as *"yoona ki-ga shimasu"* (it seems to me) and *"yoo-niomowaremasu"* (it seems to me —formal).

## (4) Reserved expressions used when stating one's convenience

In polite conversation one should show reserve when stating one's own convenience. One way is to use some preliminary remark before coming out and stating one's convenience; another is to leave the last part of the sentence unsaid.

**preliminary remarks**

a) *dekimashitara* (if possible)

To show reserve, one says *"dekimashitara"* before stating one's convenience:

> ACQUAINTANCE A: *Ja, itsu-ni shimashoo-ka.* (What day shall we make it?)
> ACQUAINTANCE B: *Ee,* **dekimashitara** *ashita-ga yoroshii-n-desu-ga.* (If possible, tomorrow would be convenient for me.)

Sometimes *"dekimashitara"* alone is used when agreeing with something.

> ACQUAINTANCE A: *Ja, ashita-ni shimashoo-ka.* (Then shall we make it tomorrow?)
> ACQUAINTANCE B: *Hai,* **dekimashitara.** (Yes, if possible.)

Similar expressions are *"yoroshikattara"* (if it suits you) and *"osashitsukae nakattara"* (if it doesn't inconvenience you). In familiar speech *"yokattara"* (if it suits you) and *"sashitsukae nakattara"* (if it doesn't inconvenience you) are used.

116

b) *katte-desu-ga* (*lit.* I'm being selfish but)

This pattern indicates that one is going to go ahead and state one's convenience although realizing it is impolite to do so.

Similar expressions are "*kattena koto-o yuu/mooshiageru yoo-desu-ga*" (*lit.* it may sound as if I am talking in a selfish way, but) and "*kattena koto-o mooshiagete sumimasen-ga*" (*lit.* I'm sorry to talk in a selfish way, but).

**reserved expressions concerning one's convenience**

a) *to tasukarimasu-ga* (it would help me if)

This is usually used with conditional expressions like "*soo shite-itadakeru-to*" (if you would do so for me):

> *Raishuu-ni shite itadakeru-to taihen tasukarimasu-ga.* (It would help me a lot if we could make it next week.)

A similar expression, "*to arigatai-n-desu-ga*" (*lit.* I would be grateful), is also used

> *Raishuu-ni shite-itadakeru-to taihen arigatai-n-desu-ga.* (It would help me a lot if we could make it next week.)

This type of expression is always followed by "*kedo*" or "*ga*" when indicating one's convenience.

b) *tara-to omoimasu-ga* (I wish)

This literally means "if . . .," the rest implying "I would be very happy" is understood and left out:

> *Raishuu-ni shite-itadaketara-to omoimasu-ga.* (It would be very good if we could make it next week.)

This also should end in "*ga*" or "*kedo*."

**trying to accommodate oneself to others**   It is polite to indicate that you will act according to the other person's wishes before actually stating your own convenience. In fact many Japanese first use such expressions when asked about their convenience:

117

*Itsu-demo kekkoo-desu.* (Any time will do.)

*Doko-demo kekkoo-desu.* (Any place will be all right with me.)

*Nan-demo kamaimasen.* (Anything will be all right with me.)

In actuality one cannot always agree to what another person wishes, and one will then have to state one's own convenience anyway, but it is regarded as childish to immediately start stating one's own convenience when asked. Thus, a reserved conversation will proceed as follows:

ACQUAINTANCE A: *Kono tsugi-wa itsu-ni shimashoo.* (When shall we meet next?)

ACQUAINTANCE B: **Itsu-demo kekkoo-desu.** (Any day will be fine.)

A: *Raishuu-no getsuyoobi-wa doo-desu-ka.* (What about next week Monday?)

B: **Soo-desu-nee** ... *getsuyoobi-wa* ... (Well, Monday isn't . . .)

A: *Ja, kayoobi.* (Tuesday, then.)

B: *Anoo,* **kattena koto-o mooshiageru yoo-desu-ga** ... (Well, I hate to be pushy, but . . .)

A: *Ie, doozo, doozo.* (Please go ahead.)

B: **Dekimashitara** *suiyoobi-ni shite-***itadakeru-to tasukari-masu-ga.** (If possible, Wednesday would be good for me.)

A: *Ii-desu-yo. Ja, suiyoobi.* (Wednesday is fine.)

B: *Doomo mooshiwake arimasen.* (Thank you — *lit.* I'm very sorry.)

### expressions used when starting discussions

a) *sassoku-desu-ga* (*lit.* it is so soon but)

It is impolite to go into business discussions without due procedure in Japan. Foreigners often complain that Japanese businessmen tend to spend too much time talking before they start business discussions. Actually, when they are forced to, they can start talking business rather quickly, but still they have the idea that one should spend sufficient time and energy in building up a good atmosphere before going into business discussions. Thus, several expressions are used in apology for having to start business discussions too quickly.

> **Sassoku-desu-ga** kono aida-no ohanashi-desu-ne ... (I sound hasty, but this is about what we discussed the other day)

b) *jitsu-wa* (as a matter of fact)

This phrase is also used when one starts discussing or explaining something. While "*sassoku-desu-ga*" is most often used when starting business discussions, "*jitsu-wa*" is used in any situation.

> ACQUAINTANCE A (after talking about the weather and general topics): **Jitsu-wa** kyoo-wa chotto onegai-ga arimashite ... (As a matter of fact, I wonder if I could ask for a favor.)
> ACQUAINTANCE B: Hai, donna koto-deshoo. (Yes, of course. What can I do for you?)

Even these days when time is valuable and people like to act quickly, it is regarded as impolite to start on what one has to say before the other person is ready.

## (5) A reserved development of conversation

**consideration toward the listener**     When talking with someone with reserve, it is most important that one uses not only reserved expressions but also a reserved development of the conversation in general. By reserved development, we mean paying special attention to how the listener feels about the talk.

Namely, you should first make sure that the listener is ready to listen. In other words, you should use the reserved expressions for addressing someone discussed earlier. And after you have started talking, it is necessary to frequently stop and ascertain that the listener understands and is ready to continue to listen. The proper use of *aizuchi* (see p. 19) plays an important role in this respect. You should always make sure, while you are speaking, that the listener is pleasantly following your talk. What matters is, in a word, your consideration toward the listener.

**proceeding step by step**    Thus, in reserved speech, one must try to proceed step by step. For instance, when you are explaining a certain matter, you should first introduce the topic as in

>*Senjitsu-no kaigi-no koto-na-n-desu-ga* . . . (This is about the last meeting.)

And when the speaker has been prepared for the next step, you can go on to further explanation, as in

>*Jitsu-wa ano kettee-ni tsuite moo ichido kangaeta-n-desu-ga.* (As a matter of fact I have been thinking the decision over.)

and wait for the listener to give *aizuchi*. One can even pause after "*Jitsu-wa ano kettee-ni tsuite*," and wait for the other person to give *aizuchi*.

Then you will go on to explain how you felt on second thought.

>*Doomo hiyoo-no ten-de mondai-ga aru yoona ki-ga suru-no-desu-ga.* (Somehow it seems to me that there is a problem in respect to the cost.)

This may seem to be overhesitant and somewhat clumsy, but in Japanese conversation it sounds more considerate and therefore polite. If you said the whole thing in one breath, as in

>*\*Senjitsu-no kaigi-no kettee-ni tsuite moo ichido kangae-te-mite, hiyoo-no ten-de mondai-ga aru-to omoimashita.*

120

it will be understood but it will not sound reserved.

To sound reserved, using expressions of reserve — such as "*no koto-desu-ga*," "*n-desu-ga*," "*doomo*" and "*yoona ki-ga suru*," as shown in the example above — is very important, but going through a step-by-step development is even more important.

## 5. The Expression of Giving and Receiving Favors

### (1) Referring to having received a favor

**readiness to acknowledge a favor** When referring to someone's action which has had some good effect on the speaker, the speaker has to use an expression acknowledging this favor. For instance, when someone has informed you about something, you should say something like

1. *Oshiete-kudasaimashita.* (He was kind enough to tell me.)
2. *Oshiete-kuremashita.* (He was kind enough to tell me.)
3. *Oshiete-itadakimashita.* (He was kind enough to tell me.)
4. *Oshiete-moraimashita.* (He was kind enough to tell me.)

Nos. 1 and 2 emphasize someone's doing a kind action and 3 and 4 emphasize the speaker's receiving kindness from someone; Nos. 1 and 3 indicate that the favor was done by a superior and 2 and 4 that it was done by an equal. However, all four express the speaker's consciousness of the doer's kindness.

If in referring to the same action of someone telling you something, you said

　　　*Oshiemashita.

or

　　　*Tanaka-san-ga watashi-ni oshiemashita.

it would sound strange. This is appropriate only when the speaker has no personal feelings towards the doer of the action or has an antipathy toward him or her.

In the same way, such statements as the following sound foreign:

5. *Tanaka-san-ga watashi-o tetsudaimashita.* (Miss Tanaka helped me.)

6. *Tanaka-san-ga watashi-ni denwa-shimashita.* (Miss Tanaka telephoned me.)

7. *Tanaka-san-ga watashi-tachi-no kodomo-no komori-o shimashita.* (Miss Tanaka did babysitting for us.)

8. *Tanaka-san-ga eki-made watashi-tachi-o okurimashita.* (Miss Tanaka walked with us to the station by way of seeing us off.)

These statements will sound all right if changed as follows:

5. *Tanaka-san-ga tetsudatte-kuremashita/kudasaimashita.*
   *Tanaka-san-ni tetsudatte-moraimashita/itadakimashita.*

6. *Tanaka-san-ga denwa-shite-kuremashita/kudasaimashita.*
   *Tanaka-san-ni denwa-shite-moraimashita/itadakimashita.*

7. *Tanaka-san-ga komori-o shite-kuremashita/kudasaimashita.*
   *Tanaka-san-ni komori-o shite-moraimashita/itadakimashita.*

8. *Tanaka-san-ga eki-made okutte-kuremashita/kudasaimashita.*
   *Tanaka-san-ni eki-made okutte-moraimashita/itadakimashita.*

It is very important to be ready to acknowledge a favor in this way; this consciousness of receiving a favor from someone is essential if you want to understand and use polite language in Japanese.

Even when the agent is not conscious of having done a favor for the speaker, the speaker will often refer to such a favor. For instance, a teacher will say something like the following about his or her student:

*Kono-goro-wa yoku benkyoo-shite-kuremasu.* (He/She studies hard these days — *lit.* He/She is doing me the favor of studying hard.)

Although the student is not studying just to please the teacher, the teacher is happy about the student's hard work, and uses *"kureru"* to indicate warm feelings toward that student.

Referring to a favor is necessary even when talking about actions in the third person; it is even more necessary when directly thanking the performer of some kindness for one.

**acknowledging a favor when thanking some-one** When thanking someone, you should be sure to use expressions of receiving a favor both in polite speech and familiar speech, as in

*Tetsudatte-kudasatte, arigatoo-gozaimashita.* (Thank you very much for helping me — polite)

*Tetsudatte-kurete, arigatoo.* (Thanks for your help — familiar)

*Tetsudatte-itadaite, arigatoo-gozaimashita.* (Thank you very much for helping me — polite)

*Tetsudatte-moratte, arigatoo.* (Thanks for your help — familiar)

You cannot say something like *"Tetsudatte, arigatoo-gozaimashita."*

To give another example, when receiving a visitor it is polite to say something like

*Yoku kite-kudasaimashita.* (Thank you very much for coming — polite)

*Yoku oide-kudasaimashita.* (Thank you very much for coming — very polite)

*Yoku kite-kureta-ne.* (Thanks for coming — familiar)

123

It is not polite to say *"*Yoku kimashita-ne.*"

**acknowledging a favor in a business situation** Even in business transactions expressions of receiving a favor are common. For instance, when talking about having consulted a doctor, you will say

Oisha-san-ni mite-itadakimashita. (I consulted a doctor — *lit.* I received the favor of seeing me from a doctor.)

In the same way:

Teepu-rekoodaa-o naoshite-moratta. (I had my tape recorder fixed — *lit.* I received the favor of fixing my tape recorder.)

Tanaka-sensee-ni nihongo-o oshiete-itadakimashita. (Prof. Tanaka taught me Japanese.)

In the above situations, the speaker paid for the service or help, but it is still common to indicate having received a favor.

**use by salespeople** People engaged in sales use expressions of the customers paying them a favor very often. For instance, instead of saying "*kore-o tsukaeba*" (if you use this), they will often say

Kore-o **otsukai-itadakeba,** motto otoku-de-gozaimasu. (If you use this, it will save you money.)

Instead of saying "*tazunetara*" (if you ask us a question), they will say

**Otazune-itadakimashitara,** kuwashiku gosetsumee-mooshiagemasu. (If you ask us, we will be glad to answer — *lit.* If we receive the favor of your asking us, we will humbly answer your questions.)

## (2) Expressions of giving and receiving concrete objects

**words corresponding to "give"** It is easier to understand

124

expressions of giving and receiving favors if one understands how the action of giving and receiving concrete objects is expressed in Japanese.

When speaking in Japanese, there is no single word corresponding to the English word "give." In other words, when referring to someone giving something, one must know who gives it to whom. Let's look at the Japanese for "I give."

**I give**     When you say "I'm giving something to him/her," there are three words from which to choose:

1. *sashiageru* (when giving something to someone of higher status)
2. *ageru* (when giving something to someone of equal status)
3. *yaru* (when giving something to someone of lower status)

Thus:

1. *Sensee-ni hana-o sashiagemashita.* (I gave flowers to the Professor.)
2. *Tomodachi-ni hana-o agemashita.* (I gave flowers to my friend.)
3. *Kodomo-ni hana-o yarimashita.* (I gave flowers to my child.)

When referring to giving something to the listener, basically you can choose a verb from the above:

1. *sashiageru* (toward someone of higher status)
   *Kore, sashiagemasu.* (I'm giving this to you.)
2. *ageru* (toward someone of equal status)
   *Kore, ageru.* (I'm giving this to you.)
3. *yaru* (toward someone of lower status)
   *Kore, yaru.* (I'm giving this to you.)

But in actual usage, one often refrains from using such direct expressions as "*sashiageru*" in the presence of a superior, and uses completely different expressions instead:

125

*Shitsuree-desu-ga   doozo.* (*lit.* I'm being rude, but please[take it].)

*Tsumaranai mono-desu-ga.* (*lit.* This is a trifling thing, but [please take it].)

Even among equals, one often avoids using "*ageru*" and chooses another expression like

*Kore, tsukatte-kudasai.* (Please use this.)

*Yoroshikattara, doozo.* (Please accept it if you'd like.)

*Kore, moratte-kurenai?* (Won't you take this?)

Incidentally, acquaintances usually use polite expressions like one would use toward a superior, and male friends and male family members use terms that one would use toward an inferior.

MAN (to a friend): *Kore, yaru-yo.*

WOMAN (to a friend): *Kore, ageru-wa.*

FATHER (to his child): *Kore, yaru-yo.*

MOTHER (to her child): *Kore, ageru-wa.*

**someone giving something to "me"**     When referring to someone giving something to oneself, the speaker chooses one of the following two verbs:

1. *kudasaru* (someone of higher status gives something to the speaker)
2. *kureru* (someone of equal/lower status gives something to the speaker)

Thus:

*Sensee-ga kudasaimashita.* (The professor gave it to me.)

*Tomodachi-ga kuremashita.* (My friend gave it to me.)

*Otooto-ga kuremashita.* (My younger brother gave it to me.)

Notice that since both *"kudasaru"* and *"kureru"* mean "give something to ME," it is not ordinarily necessary to mention *"watashi-ni."* Only when you want to emphasize "TO ME," you will say

> *Sensee-ga watashi-ni kudasaimashita.*
>
> *Otooto-ga boku-ni kureta.* (men)
>
> *Imooto-ga watashi-ni kureta.* (women/men)

Note also that you cannot use phrases like *"watashi-ni ageru"* or *"watashi-ni yaru"*; when something is given to you yourself, you must use *"kudasaru"* or *"kureru."*

**receiving something**   There are also various ways of expressing "I receive":

1. *itadaku* (when receiving something from someone of higher status)
2. *morau* (when receiving something from someone of equal/lower status)

Thus:

> *Kore-wa sensee-ni/kara itadakimashita.* (I received this from the professor.)
>
> *Kore-wa tomodachi-ni/kara moraimashita.* (I received this from my friend.)
>
> *Kore-wa otooto-ni/kara moraimashita.* (I received this from my younger brother.)

*". . .ni itadaku"* and *". . .ga kudasaru"* refer to the same situation and both are polite.

> *Sensee-ni itadakimashita.* (The professor gave it to me.)
>
> *Sensee-ga kudasaimashita.* (The professor gave it to me.)

Both show that the speaker is grateful, but with *". . .ga kudasaimashita"* the speaker emphasizes the other person's kindness,

127

whereas with "...*ni itadakimashita*" the speaker is more concerned with being the recipient of a favor. Thus, if one were to draw a distinction between the two expressions, "...*ga kudasaimashita*" corresponds to "he kindly gave it to me," whereas "...*ni itadakimashita*" corresponds to "I received from him the favor of giving it." The same distinction applies to "...*ga kureta*" and "...*ni moratta.*" (This also applies to verbs of favor following the "*te*" form, which is explained in the next section.)

**referring to other persons giving and receiving concrete objects**   We have seen how the speaker's giving and receiving something is expressed. When describing others giving and receiving something, one first decides whether or not one can identify oneself with that person.

Namely, if you are referring to someone of equal or lower status, you can use the same words you would use for yourself, as in

> *Tomodachi-ga sensee-ni hon-o sashiagemashita.* (My friend gave a book to his teacher.)

> *Otooto-ga tomodachi-ni hon-o agemashita.* (My younger brother gave a book to his friend.)

> *Otoosan-ga otooto-ni hon-o yatta.* (My father gave a book to my younger brother.)

> *Imooto-ga tomodachi-kara hon-o moratta.* (My younger sister received a book from her friend.)

> *Imooto-ga sensee-kara hon-o itadaita.* (My younger sister received a book from her teacher.)

But when referring to someone of higher status you cannot use such expressions; you have to choose a completely different wording. When your teacher gives something to another teacher, his colleague, the giving is done between equals, so you choose "*ageru,*" and since you are referring to a teacher, you use respectful expressions as in

*Tanaka-sensee-ga Yoshida-sensee-ni hon-o oage-ni nari-mashita.* (Prof. Tanaka gave a book to Prof. Yoshida.)

However, when the two teachers are not equal but are in the relation of superior and inferior, it is difficult to choose the appropriate expression because the word *"sashiageru"* is not appropriate for someone you should respect. In such cases, one avoids using expressions related to favor.

**a speaker-oriented form of expression** As can be seen from the explanations above, expressions of giving and receiving like *"ageru,"* *"kureru,"* etc., are essentially speaker-oriented. When choosing one of these, try to keep in mind that the form of expression is decided from the viewpoint of the speaker.

## (3) Expressions of doing and receiving favors

The words used for giving and receiving concrete objects are added to the *"te"* form of the verb to refer to doing and receiving favors. The use of these words based on personal relations is the same as when they are used alone.

**doing a favor for someone**

a) *te-ageru*

*"Ageru"* is used when doing something for persons equal in social status with oneself, as in

*Kore, **motte-agemashoo.*** (I'll carry it for you — said to a friend.)

b) *te-sashiageru*

*"Sashiageru"* can be added to *"te"* as in

*Kore, **motte-sashiagemashoo.***

but this is usually replaced by the more humble expression *"omochi-shimashoo."* (*cf.* p. 104)

c) *te-yaru*

*"te-yaru"* is mainly used by men; women often choose *"te-*

129

*ageru*" even when referring to doing a favor for someone lower in status.

> *Kore,* **motte-yaru**-*yo.* (I'll carry it for you — said by a man to a friend)

> *Kore,* **motte-ageru**-*wa.* (I'll carry it for you — said by a woman to a friend or by a mother to her child)

**someone else doing a favor**

a) *te-kudasaru*

"*te-kudasaru*" is used to refer to a person higher in status doing a favor for the speaker.

> *Shachoo-ga* **oshiete-kudasaimashita.** (The director told me.)

> *Sensee-ga sakubun-o* **naoshite-kudasaimashita.** (My teacher corrected my composition for me.)

b) *te-kureru*

"*te-kureru*" is used to refer to a person lower in status doing a favor for the speaker.

> *Tomodachi-ga sakubun-o* **naoshite-kuremashita.** (My friend corrected my composition for me.)

> *Otooto-ga* **oshiete-kuremashita.** (My younger brother told me.)

**receiving a favor**

a) *te-itadaku*

When someone superior in status does one a favor, "*te-itadaku*" is used, as in

> *Sensee-ni sakubun-o* **naoshite-itadakimashita.** (My teacher corrected my composition for me.)

When one is receiving something, "*kara*" and "*ni*" are used to indicate the giver as in "*sensee-ni itadaku,*" "*tomodachi-kara*

130

*morau.*" With "*te-itadaku*" and "*te-morau,*" "*ni*" is generally used.

b) *te-morau*

When someone equal in status does one a favor, "*te-morau*" is used, as in

*Tomodachi-ni sakubun-o* **naoshite-moraimashita.** (My friend corrected my composition for me.)

**expressions of favor used in requests**

a) *te-kudasaru, te-kureru*

When making a request, it is common to use "*te-kudasai-masen-ka*" and "*te-kuremasen-ka*":

*Chotto* **matte-kudasaimasen-***ka.* (Could you wait a little while? — polite)

*Chotto* **matte-kuremasen-***ka.* (Can you wait a little while? — familiar)

The affirmative forms, namely "*te-kudasaimasu-ka*" and "*te-kuremasu-ka,*" are also used in requests; the affirmative sounds more reserved and the negative more eager. In terms of frequency, "*masen-ka*" is used more often.

*Chotto* **matte-kudasaimasu-***ka.* (Could you wait a little while?)

*Chotto* **matte-kuremasu-***ka.* (Will you wait a little while?)

b) *te-itadaku, te-morau*

"*Itadaku*" and "*morau*" are used in the negative potential form in requests:

*Chotto* **oshiete-itadakemasen-***ka.* (Could you help me? — *lit.* Could you teach me?)

*Chotto* **oshiete-moraemasen-***ka.* (Can you help me?)

131

You should be careful in pronouncing the "$e$" sound before "-$masen$" here; if it sounds like "$i$," the sentence will not make sense.

The affirmative forms "$te$-$itadakemasu$-$ka$" and "$te$-$moraemasu$-$ka$" can be used as well, but the negative forms are more usual. The difference between the two is similar to that between "$te$-$kudasaimasu$-$ka$" and "$te$-$kudasaimasen$-$ka$" explained above.

The pattern "$te$-$itadaku/morau$" is also used in requests in the form of "$te$-$itadakitai/moraitai$-$n$-$desu$-$ga$." You can make a request polite by adding "$tai$-$n$-$desu$-$ga$," as in

Chotto **oshiete-itadakitai-n-desu-ga.** (Could you help me? — *lit.* I'd like to be taught but.)

Chotto **oshiete-moraitai-n-desu-ga.** (less polite)

The "$ga$" here can be replaced by "$kedo$"; "$ga$" sounds more formal. (*cf.* p. 117)

c) "$o$" plus stem plus "$kudasaimasen/itadakemasen$-$ka$"

The pattern "$o$" plus stem is used with "$kudasaimasen$-$ka$" or "$itadakemasen$-$ka$" in place of the "$te$" form.

Shooshoo omachi-**kudasaimasen-ka.** (Could you wait for a little while?)

Shooshoo omachi-**itadakemasen-ka.** (Could you wait for a little while?)

Sometimes this is used with "$kudasaimasu$-$ka$" or "$itadakemasu$-$ka$," but it cannot be used with "$kuremasen$-$ka$" or "$moraemasen$-$ka$."

132

# PART III CONCERN FOR OTHERS

## 1. Polite Language and Human Relations

Needless to say, polite language is used to establish and maintain good human relations. One tries to always use the proper respectful expressions, humble expressions, and reserved expresssions in one's contacts with other persons. But to maintain good personal relations, one should also express friendliness and a concern for others.

When hearing about Japanese politeness, it may seem to foreigners that the Japanese are always guarding a careful distance from others. This is not the case. The Japanese language is rich in expressions of friendliness and concern. In fact, the most important factor in polite language is consideration toward others. We will discuss how the Japanese express their friendliness and concern in the following sections.

## 2. The Expression of Friendliness and Intimacy

(1) The use of particles

Several sentence particles are used in conversation to express the speaker's feelings and attitude toward the listener.

a) *ne*

"*Ne*" is used to show agreement; it is also used when one expects the listener to agree.

*Honto-ni soo-desu-ne.* (That's certainly true, isn't it?)

A:   *Ii otenki-desu-**ne**.* (Lovely day, isn't it?)

B:   *Ee, soo-desu-**ne**.* (Yes, isn't it?)

A:   *Kore-de juubun-deshoo-**ne**.* (This is enough, don't you think?)

B:   *Saa, chotto tarinai-kamo shiremasen.* (Well, it may be a little insufficient.)

In example 1, the speaker is agreeing with what the other person has said. In example 2, speaker A expects B to agree, and B does agree. Both of them use "*ne*." In example 3, the speaker is trying to make sure that B agrees, but B disagrees.

As can be seen in the examples above, the particle "*ne*" is used to show the speaker's concern with the listener's agreement. "*Ne*" is used surprisingly frequently between two people who are on good terms with each other.

Sometimes "*ne*" is used at the end of a phrase, as well as at the end of a sentence, as in

*Kinoo-**ne**, kaisha-e ittara-**ne**, Yamada-san-ga saki-ni kite-ite-**ne**, watashi-no kao-o miru-to-**ne** . . .* (Yesterday, when I went to the office, Mr. Yamada was already there, and when he saw me . . .)

*Ima chotto-**ne**, isogashii-kara-**ne**, sono hen-de-**ne** shibaraku matte-te-kurenai?* (Right now I'm sort of busy, so would you mind waiting for me a while there?)

This repeated use of "*ne*" shows that the speaker is anxious to have the listener listen and agree; therefore this usage is primarily seen in familiar conversation. Adding "*ne*" once at the end of a sentence which ends politely, as in

*Osamuku narimashita-**ne**.* (It has become cold, hasn't it?)

is polite, but using "*ne*" between phrases shows familiarity.

134

"*Ne*" can also be used with other sentence particles such as "*yo*," "*wa*," "*no*" and "*ka*."

*Kore-de juubun-desu-***yone**. (This is enough, don't you think?)

*Ara, kore, ii-***wane**. (Oh, this is nice, isn't it?)

*Kore-de ii-***none**. (This is all right, isn't it?)

*Chotto mazui-n-ja nai-desu-***kane**. (Isn't this a little bit defective?)

Since "*ne*" shows the speaker's concern toward the listener, it always comes after the other particle; you cannot reverse the order of the particles in the last four examples.

b) *yo*

While "*ne*" indicates that the speaker feels the same way as the listener, "*yo*" shows that the speaker wants to emphasize his or her own judgment regardless of how the listener feels. Thus, the two are completely different. The figures below show the difference.

ne

yo

listener   speaker          listener   speaker

While saying "*ne*" the speaker is emotionally going closer to the listener; while saying "*yo*," the speaker is emotionally pulling the listener toward himself.

When "*omoshiroi-desu-ne*" is used, for instance, both the speaker and the listener are expected to feel interested; on the other

135

hand, when speakers use "*omoshiroi-desu-yo*," they are trying to impress their own judgment on the listener, regardless of how the listener may feel.

Because of this, "*yo*" is used for maintaining good relations only when the speaker is trying to put the listener at ease, as in

A: *Daijoobu-deshoo-ka*. (I wonder if it is all right.)
B: *Daijoobu-desu-yo*. (I'm sure it is all right.)

A: *Doomo sumimasen*. (I'm very sorry.)
B: *Iie, kamaimasen-yo*. (No, no. Don't worry about it.)

In the examples above, "*yo*" is more considerate and appropriate then "*ne*."

Sometimes "*yo*" and "*ne*" are used together as in

*Kore-de juubun-desu-yone*.

In this case, the speaker first emphasizes his or her own judgment, and then expresses an expectation of the listener's agreement.

c) *no*

The sentence particle "*no*" is used in two different ways; one is to indicate a question as in

1. *Kyoo-wa doko-e iku-no*. (Where are you going today?)

and the other is to explain a situation or to emphasize one's opinion, as in

2. *Kyoo-wa massugu kaeru-no*. (I'm going straight home today.)

In fact, the former (no. 1) is the abbreviation of "*no-desu-ka*" and the latter that of "*no-desu*." Both are used in familiar conversation.

The former usage can be observed among both men and women, but since it sounds rather soft and gentle, it is used more often by women. Men use it more often when speaking with women than when speaking with men. When speaking to children, both men and women use it with equal frequency. In other words, this "*no*" shows a kind and considerate attitude towards a weaker person.

On the other hand, the second usage of "*no*," as in no. 2, is almost entirely limited to women and children; men use it only when speaking to women and children.

The two usages look exactly the same in writing, but are distinguished in speech by a rising or falling tone.

$$no?$$
*Kore-kara doko-e iku* ↗ (question)
*Kyoo-wa massugu kaeru* ↘ (explanation)
$$no.$$

d) *ka*

The particle "*ka*" at the end of a sentence forms a question, of course. But sentences ending with "*ka*" are not always meant to be questions. In conversation they are often used to show that the listener has understood what the other person has said. "*Soo-desu-ka*" is perhaps most common, but other sentences are used in the same way.

A: *Ichijikan kakarimasu-yo.* (It will take an hour [to get there].)

B: *Ichijikan-desu-***ka***. Ja, moo dekakenakya.* (One hour? Then I have to leave now.)

B will pronounce "*ka*" with a rising tone when making sure and with a falling tone when showing understanding.

Sometimes even a fairly long sentence is repeated:

A: *Ichijikan kakarimasu-yo.*

B: *Ichijikan kakarimasu-***ka***. Ja, moo dekakenakya.*

Sometimes "*n-desu-ka*" is used to show that the speaker is considering the fact.

A: *Ichijikan kakarimasu-yo.*

137

B:   *Ichijikan kakaru-**n-desu-ka**. Ja, moo dekake-nakya.*

In familiar conversation, plain forms are used:

A:   *Ichijikan kakaru-yo.*
B:   *Ichijikan-**ka**. Ja, . . .*
*Ichijikan kakaru-**ka**. Ja, . . .*
*Ichijikan kakaru-**no-ka**. Ja, . . .*

Women omit "*ka*" in familiar conversation:

B:   *Ichijikan. Ja, . . .*
*Ichijikan kakaru. Ja, . . .*
*Ichijikan kakaru-no. Ja, . . .*

This question-like statement plays an important role in conversation. If you listen closely, you will find that the Japanese make this type of statement frequently. One foreigner noticed this once when speaking with a Japanese acquaintance and wondered if his pronunciation were unclear, but this was not the case. The Japanese use this statement to show that they are listening attentively and have understood what was said; in a sense this is like *aizuchi*. Foreigners should not be annoyed or worried when their Japanese listeners do this. And if they can go ahead and do the same thing themselves, they will be accepted more warmly by the Japanese.

e) other sentence particles

i) *wa*

"*Wa*" is used mainly by women to emphatically state a judgment (*cf.* pp. 73-4) as in

*Sonna koto arimasen-**wa**.* (That's not true — polite)

*Sonna koto nai-**wa**.* (That's not true — familiar)

To show the speaker's concern about the listener, "*ne*" is added to "*wa*" as in

*Omoshirokatta-desu-**wane**.* (It was interesting, wasn't it? — polite)

138

*Omoshirokatta-**wane**.* (It was interesting, wasn't it? — familiar)

*Kore-de daijoobu-desu-**wane**.* (This is all right, isn't it? — polite)

When the speaker wants to add emphasis, "*yone*" is added:

*Kore-de daijoobu-desu-**wa-yone**.* (This is all right, don't you think? — polite)

*Kore-de daijoobu-da-**wa-yone**.* (This is all right, don't you think? — familiar)

Although women use "*wa*" in both polite and familiar conversation, they use it more often in familiar conversation.

Men sometimes use "*wa*" for emphasis, but this is limited to older men, and is especially prevalent in the Kansai district.

ii) *na*

"*Na*" is usually used when talking to oneself as in

*Samui-**na**. Dekakeru-no, iya-da-**na**.* (It's cold! I don't want to go out!)

But when talking to younger people or to someone of lower status "*na*" is added to commands and instructions:

*Ii-**na**. Owattara sugu kaette-kuru-n-da-yo.* (Come back as soon as it's finished. Okay?)

*Ii-ka. Wakatta-**na**.* (Okay? Understand?)

Adding "*ka*" gives a more reserved tone:

*Ii-ka. Wakatta-**ka-na**.* (Okay? Do you understand?)

This usage of "*na*" is limited to men's familiar speech; women use "*wane*" in similar situations.

*Ii-**wane**. Owattara sugu kaette-kuru-no-yo.*

*Ii? Wakatta-***wane***.*

iii) *ya*

"*Ya*" is sometimes used for casual emphasis in familiar conversation; it is used mainly by men.

> HUSBAND: *Nanika taberu mono nai?* (Is there anything to eat?)
> WIFE: *Omochi-ga aru-kedo.* (We have some rice cakes.)
> HUSBAND: *Mochi? Un, sore-wa-ii-***ya***.* (Rice cakes? Good!)

iv) *ze* and *zo*

In very familiar conversation, "*ze*" and "*zo*" are used in a similar way to "*yo*"; "*zo*" is stronger and more aggressive than "*ze*." Women seldom use these even in very familiar speech.

## (2) The use of kinship terms

**use by children**　　The Japanese use kinship terms with non-family members to show intimacy. This is especially common among young children. They usually address and refer to non-family members and strangers with kinship terms alone or added to a personal name. Thus they will use "*ojisan*" (uncle) and "*obasan*" (aunt) when referring to adults.

> *Otonari-no ***ojisan***-wa Yamada-to iimasu.* (*lit.* The uncle next door is Mr. Yamada.)

> *Ano ***obasan***-wa ii hito-desu.* (*lit.* That aunt is a nice person.)

> *Henna ***ojisan***-ni hanashikakerareta.* (A strange man spoke to me.)

Sometimes they add the name of the person and "*-no*";

> *Kore-wa Yamada-san-***no*** ***obasan***-ni moratta-no.* (Mrs. Yamada gave this to me — *lit.* I received it from Auntie at the Yamadas.)

They use "*oniisan*" (older brother) and "*oneesan*" (older sister) when addressing or referring to young people older than themselves.

*Otonari-no* **oneesan**-*ga daigaku-ni haitta*. (*lit*. Older sister next door has entered college.)

**Oniisan***, totte*. (when asking a young man living in the neighborhood to catch a ball)

**use by adults**    Sometimes adults adopt this usage of kinship terms; they will at times address younger people they do not know as "*oniisan*" or "*oneesan*" and elderly persons as "*ojiisan*" (grandfather) or "*obaasan*" (grandmother), as in:

*A,* **ojiisan***, abunai-desu-yo*. (Hey, watch out — *lit*. Oh, grandfather, it's dangerous.)

**Obaasan***, kono densha-desu-yo*. (Here comes your train — *lit*. Grandmother, it's this train.)

However this is not regarded as very polite.

People used to address restaurant employees with "*Oniisan!*" (Waiter!) and "*Oneesan!*" (Waitress!). This is not popular now; "*Sumimasen!*" is used instead.

## (3) An emphasis on being together

**are**    While "*kore*" (this) refers to something that is close to the speaker, and "*sore*" to something close to the listener, "*are*" refers to something that is rather far from both the speaker and listener. Using "*are*" presupposes that both the speaker and listener know or can see the object. Words starting with "*a*" — some others are "*ano*," "*asoko*," and "*achira*" — are all used in this way.

Since "*are*" presupposes that the speaker and the listener share a knowledge of the subject matter, it is used more often among people who belong to the same group. It is often used without any direct mention of what it refers to among work colleagues or within the family. For example,

> COLLEAGUE A: *Are, doo narimashita-ka.* (What happened to that?)
> COLLEAGUE B: *Aa, are-wa kaiketsu-shimashita-yo.* (Oh, that's been settled.)

Or a father may say to his children

> *Are, motte-kite.* (Bring me that.)

and the children will understand what he is referring to.

In a sense such words as *"are," "ano-hito"* and *"asoko"* are used as a sign of the speaker and the listener both having the same knowledge or experience. People like to feel that the other person has the same experiences and the same feelings. These *"a"* words are thus one indication of intimacy.

**te-kuru** *"te-kuru,"* (literally "do something and come") is often used in daily life to emphasize the speaker's being together with the listener. *"te-kuru"* is used to indicate (1) change up to the present, (2) coming after having done something, and (3) the speaker's wish to share an experience with the listener.

1. *Dandan samuku **natte-kimashita**-ne.* (It has become colder these days.)
2. *Chotto otsukai-ni **itte-kimasu**.* (I'm going out on an errand for a while.)
3. *Kinoo Shinjuku-de eega-o **mite-kimashita**.* (I saw a movie in Shinjuku yesterday.)

Of these three, 2 and 3 are used to emphasize being together.

a) *"te-kuru"* meaning "do and  come"

*"Kuru"* is usually added to words meaning "go away" like *"iku," "dekakeru"* (go out) and *"deru"* (leave). For instance, when one goes to work or to study, he says to his family

142

*Itte-kimasu*. (Bye — *lit*. I will go and come back.)

It is also usual to add "*kuru*" when one leaves home for a while to go shopping or to do an errand, as in

*Chotto sanpo-ni* **itte-kimasu**. (I'm going out for a walk.)

*Sanjippun-bakari* **dekakete-kuru**. (I'm going out for about 30 minutes.)

*Isoide* **katte-kimashoo**. (I'll go and buy it in a hurry.)

And when one returns, one says

*Itte-kimashita*. (I'm back — *lit*. I've gone and come back.)

*Katte-kimashita-yo*. (I bought it — *lit*. I've bought it and come back.)

This "*kuru*" is most often observed between family members, and also at places of work where people feel they belong to the same group. Depending on the job, employees may say either

*Shokuji-ni ikimasu.* (I'm going out for lunch.)

or

*Shokuji-ni* **itte-kimasu**. (I'm going out for lunch.)

The difference depends on how close they feel towards their colleagues.

b) "*te-kuru*" indicating a desire to share an experience

When telling someone about an experience, one says either

*Kono-aida Fujisan-ni* **nobotte-kimashita**. (I climbed Mt. Fuji the other day.)

or

*Kono-aida Fujisan-ni noborimashita*. (I climbed Mt. Fuji the other day.)

In the second sentence, the speaker does not sound eager to talk

143

about this experience. If *"nobotte-kimashita"* is used, the listener is signaled to be ready to listen and to say something like

> *Sore-de* . . . (And then [what happened]?)

rather than simply saying

> *Soo-desu-ka*. (Is that right?)

Because *"te-kuru"* has this effect on the listener, speakers sometimes make conscious use of it. For instance, a lecturer will say to an audience

> *Senjitsu Chuugoku-e **itte-mairimashita**-ga* . . . (I went to China the other day and . . .)

(*"Mairimashita"* sounds more humble than *"kimashita."*) By using this pattern, the speaker can convey a sense of eagerness to talk about this experience.

## 3. The Expression of Concern

### (1) Daily expressions

An English-speaking person might express concern toward another by asking "How are you?" or "How are things going?" The Japanese also express their concern about others, but in somewhat different ways.

**ogenki-desu-ka** *"Ogenki-desu-ka"* (*lit.* Are you well?) may correspond to the English "How are you?" as far as the verbal meaning is concerned, but these two actually differ in usage. While "How are you?" does not necessarily ask whether the other person is really healthy or not, *"Ogenki-desu-ka"* still has some of this literal meaning. Therefore *"Ogenki-desu-ka"* is used only when two people have not met for some time, and really do not know how the other has been. It is strange to say *"Ogenki-desu-ka"* to persons you meet every day unless you have noticed some

144

remarkable change in them. *"Gokigen ikaga-desu-ka"* and *"Ikaga-desu-ka"* are used in the same way; however, these sound more formal.

The following are also used to express one's concern when meeting someone whom one has not seen for some time.

*Kono-goro-wa doo-desu-ka.* (How are you these days?)

*Oshigoto-wa doo-desu-ka.* (How is your work going?)

*Keeki-wa doo-desu-ka.* (How is your business going?)

To express concern when *"Ogenki-desu-ka"* or its like are not appropriate, one uses completely different expressions.

**referring to the weather** The Japanese often refer to the weather when they meet. Although they are not referring to each other's health directly, they are expressing their concern for the other because the weather is a mutual concern.

Such reference to the weather always ends in *"(-desu)-ne,"* as in

*Ii otenki-desu-ne.* (Lovely weather, isn't it?)

*Iyana otenki-desu-ne.* (Disagreeable weather, isn't it?)

*Samui-desu-ne.* (It's cold, isn't it?)

*Suzushikute, tasukarimasu-ne.* (It's nice and cool, isn't it? — *lit.* It is cool and helps us, doesn't it?)

*Yoku furimasu-ne.* (It surely rains /snows a lot, doesn't it?)

And the other person usually repeats the same sentence or gives a slightly modified version as in

A: *Ii otenki-desu-ne.*
B: *Ee, honto-ni ii otenki-desu-ne.*

It may seem to foreigners as if the Japanese don't like to directly show concern toward each other, but actually reference to the weather is an indirect expression of concern.

145

**dochira-e?** Sometimes a neighbor will ask a question like

Dochira-e? (*lit.* To where?)

Dochira-e odekake-desu-ka. (*lit.* Where are you going?)

These are not literal questions but expressions of concern. The Japanese ask where others are going because they want to know whether they should be happy about their being healthy and wealthy enough to go out to have fun or whether they should be worried about their having to go out to attend to some business. At any rate, the questioner is not really interested in the exact destination, so the answer to this type of question is:

Ee, chotto sono hen-made. (Yes, I'm just going down the street a little way.)

One does not have to tell exactly where one is going.

This type of exchange is common where people live in a small community and know each other personally. In big cities where people in a neighborhood do not have such personal relations, this type of question is not often asked.

"Odekake-desu-ka" (Are you going out?) is also used in the same way. This seems to be more common then "Dochira-e," which many now feel to be a little too intrusive.

**itte-rasshai** "Itte-rasshai" literally means "Please go and come back." This is said by a family member to another family member who is going out, and the person going out says

Itte-kimasu. (I'm going and coming back.)

Itte-mairimasu. (I'm going and coming back — more formal)

People in a family never say "Sayonara" (Good-bye) to each other. When parting temporarily they always refer to coming back to each other.

146

This type of exchange is also used by neighbors or colleagues when they feel they have a family-like relationship.

Incidentally, *"konnichiwa"* (hi; good day) and *"konbanwa"* (good evening) are also not used between family members. Sometimes foreigners staying with a Japanese family say *"Konnichiwa"* or *"Sayonara"* to them, and this can be the cause of ill feelings. Actually one American reports that she was scolded by the grandfather of the family when she said *"Konbanwa"* to him. (However, *"oyasumi-nasai"* and *"ohayoo-gozaimasu"* are used between family members.)

When arriving home, one is greeted by

*Okaeri-nasai.* (Welcome home.)

One then says

*Tadaima.* (I'm home — *lit.* Right now.)

And this exchange also occurs between colleagues and neighbors when they feel they enjoy family-like relations.

**referring to previous meetings** The Japanese also feel it is important to refer to previous meetings when meeting again. If the other person treated you to something to drink or eat, you should say

*Senjitsu-wa gochisoosama-deshita.* (Thank you for the nice treat the other day.)

If you just met without eating or drinking, or if you are the one who paid, you should say

*Senjitsu-wa shitsuree-(ita)shimashita.* (*lit.* I was rude the other day.)

In less formal conversation you can just say

*Senjitsu-wa doomo.*

147

or *Kono-aida-wa doomo.* (familiar)

Sometimes foreigners do not do this because they think they thanked the other sufficiently at the time, but negligence of this custom is regarded as rude by the Japanese. Even if you already thanked your Japanese acquaintance appropriately at your previous meeting, you should be sure to express gratitude again at your next meeting.

Behind this custom is the underlying idea that it is important for two persons to both share an experience and express an awareness of sharing it. They want to feel that they have had good relations from some time before.

**doozo yoroshiku** When two people are introduced to each other for the first time, they say

*Hajimemashite. Doozo yoroshiku.* (Glad to meet you.)

"*Doozo yoroshiku*" literally means "please treat me in a good way." This serves to show the speaker's wish to maintain good relations with the other person.

"*Doozo yoroshiku*" is used when one asks others to do something, and they have agreed to do so; in this case it means "please take good care of the matter for me." In English one will say "Thank you" in such cases, but in Japanese this phrase is added, as in

A: *Ja, soo shimashoo.* (I'll do it.)
B: *Arigatoo-gozaimasu. Doozo yoroshiku (onegai-shi-masu).*

"*Onegai-shimasu*" is added to make it very polite.

Sometimes "*doozo*" and "*yoroshiku*" are reversed when asking someone to take care of some business:

*Yoroshiku doozo.*

148

## (2) Season's greetings

**New Year's Day** New Year's Day is the most important day in Japan, as Christmas is in other countries. On this day, people used to visit each other and exchange greetings, but nowadays it is more common to send New Year's cards instead. On the cards they write their joy at the coming of the New Year and their hopes for the well-being of the other throughout the year.

The first three days of January are official holidays; on those days and until the middle of the month the Japanese exchange the following expressions whenever they meet:

*Akemashite omedetoo-gozaimasu.* (Happy New Year!)

and then

*Kotoshi-mo yoroshiku onegai-shimasu.* (*lit.* Please be good to me this year too.)

To be more polite, the following sentence is inserted between the two.

*Sakunen-juu-wa iroiro osewa-ni narimashita.* (Thank you for your many kindnesses to me last year.)

**midsummer cards** Many Japanese also send cards during the hottest season of the year, namely in July and August. Although this custom is not as general as sending New Year's cards, it is regarded as important to inquire after each other's health in the hot season. But there are no specific oral expressions used during this season.

## (3) Compliments

To say nice things about others is another way of showing concern. The Japanese, however, refrain from personal compliments when they have to be polite. The types of compliments used in polite situations are rather limited, and it is customary for the person complimented to deny all compliments.

149

**compliments on someone's residence** Compliments on a person's home are common, even in polite situations. A visitor will usually say something like

*Ii osumai-desu-ne.* (You have a very nice house.)

And the host/ess will deny this

*Iie.* (No, no.)

and often talk about weak points such as being located in an inconvenient place or being in a noisy neighborhood.

**compliments on one's family** Complimenting others on their children is very common; the younger the children, the easier it is to offer such compliments. Common expressions are

*Ii okosan-desu-ne.* (You have a very nice child.)

*Kawaii okosan-desu-ne.* (He/She is a lovely child.)

*Kashikosoona okosan-desu-ne.* (He/She looks very clever.)

People do not freely compliment adult members of a family, however, unless they are very old. In fact, it is the weaker members of a family that can be complimented most safely.

The response to such compliments is usually "*Iie,*" and a detailing of the weak points of one's children as in

*Itazura-de komarimasu.* (He/She does not behave very well — *lit.* He/She is very mischievous and troubles us.)

**compliments on possessions** It is not as common to compliment others on their possessions; in polite situations people refrain from directly praising personal possessions. However, such remarks are exchanged among people who know each other well. Work colleagues, for instance, will sometimes say such things as:

*Ii tokee-da-ne.* (You have a nice watch on.)

*Ii nekutai-da-ne.* (You have a nice tie on.)

150

But it is good to show one's concern for the other's feelings in some other way. In the above cases, one should thank the lecturer or teacher by saying

*Taihen benkyoo-ni narimashita.* (It was very instructive — *lit.* It became a great study for me.)

*Okagesama-de yoku wakarimashita.* (Thank you for your good teaching — *lit.* Thanks to you, I understood very well.)

*Ii kaban-desu-ne.* (That's a very good purse/attache case, etc.)

**compliments on clothes or appearance** The Japanese do not usually refer to a person's personal appearance unless they know each other very well. Saying something like

*Kyoo-wa totemo kiree-da-ne.* (You look very attractive today.)

is limited to good friends. To be polite, one will choose less direct expressions such as

*Ii doresu-desu-ne.* (You have a nice dress on.)

*Sono fuku oniai-desu-yo.* (That outfit suits you very well.)

**compliments on abilities** It is not common for the Japanese to praise someone's abilities, except between good friends or to someone younger. It is particularly outside the bounds of good manners to compliment superiors on their abilities. One should refrain from saying something like

*Ojoozu-desu-ne.* (You're very good at it.)

or

*Yoku dekimashita-ne.* (You did very well.)

to someone of higher age or status.

151

**compliments and the expression of concern** We have seen that the Japanese generally refrain from complimenting someone directly. It is, however, good to compliment someone indirectly. For instance, it is not polite to say to a superior about a lecture

*Joozu-ni shimashita. (You did it well.)

And it is also inappropriate for students to compliment teachers on their teaching technique as in

*Sensee, joozu-ni oshiemashita. (You taught well.)

(4) Wishing well

English is rich in expressions for wishing someone well. To give a few examples, English-speaking people often say things like "Good luck," "Have a good time," "Have a nice weekend," and "Bon voyage." Japanese have no such set expressions with the exception of

Yoi otoshi-o (omukae-kudasai). (I wish you a happy new year; said toward the end of the year)

Some people, including radio and television announcers, use such expressions as

Yoi shuumatsu-o (osugoshi-kudasai). (Have a good weekend.)

but this is not common. When people part for the weekend, they simply say

Ja, mata. (lit. See you again.)

**oki-o tsukete** To someone going on a trip, the Japanese usually say "Itte-rasshai" (lit. Please go and come back — cf. p. 146) or "Oki-o tsukete" (Please be careful) as an expression of concern.

152

THE EXPRESSION OF CONCERN

**ogenki-de** To someone who is going to be away for a long time, they often say

(Doozo) ogenki-de. (lit. Please be well.)

When a colleague departs after being transferred to a higher position, people often cry out

Banzai! (Hurrah!)

just as they do when their team has won a game.

**oraku-ni** For making a visitor feel at home, the host/ess will say

Doozo oraku-ni. (Make yourself comfortable.)

And when urging that one go ahead and help oneself to food or drink, they will say

Doozo goenryo naku. (Please don't be reserved.)

And when urging a guest to enjoy a hot bath, they will say

Doozo goyukkuri. (Please take your time.)

**wishing good luck** To a person who is going to take an examination or start some difficult work, one often says

Ganbatte-kudasai. (Stick to it.)

Shikkari yatte-ne. (Try hard.)

There are no set equivalents for the English expressions "Good luck" or "Take it easy."

To encourage a person in such a case, the Japanese say various things depending on the situation, as in

Daijoobu-desu-kara. (I'm sure you can do it well.)

Ooen-shite-ru-yo. (We'll be cheering you on.)

153

## (5) Congratulations and sympathy

**omedetoo-gozaimasu** *"Omedetoo-gozaimasu"* is always used when congratulating someone. One often states the occasion and then adds *"omedetoo-gozaimasu"* as in

> *Otanjoobi omedetoo(-gozaimasu).* (Happy birthday.)

> *(Go)nyuugaku omedetoo(-gozaimasu).* (Congratulations on entering college.)

> *(Go)kekkon omedetoo(-gozaimasu).* (Congratulations on your wedding.)

Very often just *"omedetoo"* (familiar) or *"omedetoo-gozaimasu"* (polite) is sufficient when the occasion is obvious. To be very formal one says

> *Kono tabi-wa makoto-ni omedetoo-gozaimasu.* (*lit.* Congratulations on this occasion.)

And the other person always answers

> *Arigatoo(-gozaimasu).*

and often adds

> *Minasama-no okage-desu.* (I should thank everybody — *lit.* It has become possible thanks to everybody's kindness.)

**taihen-desu-ne** The most commonly used expression of sympathy is *"taihen-desu-ne."* When you hear that the other person has to work hard or go through some difficult situation, you will say

> *Taihen-desu-ne.* (That's hard; That's tough.)

Students will say this to their friends studying hard for an examination, and workers will say this to their colleagues who have to work overtime. The response made to this expression of sympathy

154

depends on the situation; people say things like

*Ganbarimasu*. (I'll try hard.)

*Daijoobu-desu-yo*. (Don't worry.)

*Doomo*. (Thanks.)

**zannen-deshita-ne**    On hearing that someone has had a business failure, done poorly on an exam, or lost some sort of match, you should say

*Zannen-deshita-ne*. (That's too bad.)

When hearing about someone having lost belongings or money, you can say

*Oshii koto-o shimashita-ne*. (That was a pity — *lit*. You did something regrettable.)

**goshinpai-desu-ne**    To show sympathy for someone who is worrying about a family member who is ill or the like, you should say

*Goshinpai-desu-ne*. (*lit*. You must be worrying.)

**sore-wa ikemasen-ne**    When others are suffering from illness or some physical injury, or someone in their family is, you should say

*Sore-wa ikemasen-ne*. (That's too bad — *lit*. That won't do.)

and add

*Doozo odaiji-ni*. (Please take good care of yourself; I hope he's better soon, etc.)

**condolences**    To express sympathy to the bereaved, the most common set expressions are

*Goshuushoosama-desu*. (My deepest condolences.)
and

*Kokoro-kara okuyami-mooshiagemasu*. (Let me express my deepest condolences.)

It is regarded as good to be rather quiet on sad occasions. Such expressions of condolence should be said in a low, almost inaudible voice. One should also bow deeply. In fact, one sometimes bows so deeply while speaking that the second part of the sentence cannot be heard clearly. Looking and speaking sadly is more important than sounding eloquent on such occasions.

**offering help**     In case of misfortune or bereavement, one should also, of course, offer one's help. Expressions used in such cases are:

*Nanika watashi-ni dekiru koto-ga arimashitara, doozo (osshatte-kudasai).* (Please tell me if there is anything I can do for you — "*osshatte-kudasai*" is often left out.)

*Nanika otetsudai-dekiru koto-ga arimashitara, doozo goenryo naku (osshatte-kudasai).* (If there is anything I can do to help you, please feel free to tell me.)

# INDEX

# INDEX